kids' party ideas

MARKS &
SPENCER

kids' party ideas

Party Themes by Marion Haslam
Party Cakes by Carol Deacon

Marion Haslam

A freelance writer and editor of *Popular Patchwork* magazine, Marion greatly enjoys seasonal and birthday celebrations, plus the planning and 'theatre' of a successful party. Previously a buyer for several design-led retailers in the UK and abroad, Marion is also the author of *Retro Style – 50s Decorating for Today* in association with *Living etc* magazine. Other family craft books include *My Bead Box* and *Spooky Fun*.

Carol Deacon

Other titles by Carol Deacon: *Quick & Easy Novelty Cakes*, *No-Time Party Cakes*, *Party Cakes For Children*, *Sporty Cakes* and *Things to Make and Do*. For more information or to contact Carol Deacon, e-mail her at caroldeacon@hotmail.com or visit her website: www.caroldeacon.com.

Marks and Spencer p.l.c.
PO Box 3339, Chester, CH99 9QS
www.marksandspencer.com

Designed, produced and packaged by
Stonecastle Graphics Limited
Cover design by Shelley Doyle

Party themes text by Marion Haslam
Party cakes text by Carol Deacon
Costumes and craft items by Marion Haslam
Party cakes designs by Carol Deacon
Edited by Gillian Haslam
Designed by Sue Pressley and Paul Turner
Photography by Roddy Paine

ISBN 1-84461-229-5

Printed in Singapore

Marion's Acknowledgements

Special thanks to family and friends who shared their party memories and to Artworker Art Materials for the loan of the pirate chest. Dedicated with love to Alice, aged 8, experienced party-goer, fabulous fairytale princess and the best-ever niece.

DISCLAIMER
• Young children should always be supervised by a responsible adult when making the craft and food items described in this book. Adults should ensure that activities are properly set up and supervised to ensure safety and enjoyment for the party giver and guests.
• Candles are an important part of birthday traditions. Remember never to place or light candles near to paper decorations, or leave lit candles unattended. Always ask an adult to light candles and place nightlights in a suitable container. If using fairy lights to decorate the garden, make sure that they are suitable for outdoor use.
• Use either metric OR imperial measurements when baking. Do not combine both.
• Young children should never be left unsupervised if hot ovens or potentially dangerous implements such as knives or scissors are in use.
• Every effort has been taken to make the instructions clear and accurate.
• The author, publisher and their agents cannot accept liability for any loss, damage, illness or injury however caused.

CONTENTS

Kids' Parties

Inspirational ideas for planning a fabulous
party and the perfect party cake

PARTY INSPIRATION

Whether you view birthday parties as the social event of your year or an occasion to be survived probably depends whether you are the child involved or the obliging parent **organizing the whole event! However, with some inspiration** and a little lateral thinking, some help from the intended **party person and a high degree of forward planning, parties** can be enjoyed by all involved.

This book should be regarded as your saviour and stress-remover!

The following pages give some useful hints and tips on forward planning. With ideas galore for themed parties, each theme has suggestions for fantastic party cakes, easy-to-make (or adapt) costumes, invitations, games and ideas for setting the scene. You can follow this basic 'recipe' for any theme you think up. Help and ideas from your child should be welcomed at this stage with open arms. Children love to feel involved and are sure to have bright ideas of their own. After all, they are princesses and pirates on a daily basis! Plus, from a practical point of view, they can help with the preparation of invitations or table settings well in advance of the actual day.

As you know, for children the countdown to a birthday starts about three months in advance of the actual date, as soon as they pass the magical 3/4 mark each year. So why not harness some of their boundless energy when it gets to about birthday minus 6 weeks, as you are going to hear about it anyway?

PRINCESS PARTIES AND SUPER SLEEPOVERS

SENSATIONAL SUMMER PARTIES

'I'M GOING TO BE SEVEN SOON!'

Party planning hints will help you to create a birthday battle plan and suggest that you record ideas for future years. In my family, the exercise book containing details of my parties as a small child is much treasured (and slightly battered), as it records the important events in my own family's history. So, parents, pour yourself a glass of wine as you sit back and read through. On the great day you will be prepared for anything and can relax and enjoy the experience.

ARTY PARTY

WILD WILD WEST PARTY

PIRATE PARTY

PLANNING THE PERFECT PARTY

OK, let's get one thing straight – parties don't have to be perfect in order to be fabulous, memorable and a great deal of fun.

The main thing to remember is that everyone is there to have a good time, maybe dress up, play some games, get over-excited, eat some food and if you are lucky, calm down a little before they disappear off home again.

Of course, events and activities cannot (and should not) be planned with the precision of a business conference, but a little forethought saves stress (yours) and tears (theirs) on the big day. Thinking ahead also means children's parties need not be expensive, as creative home-based and home-made parties will often contain the most original and memorable ideas. After all, anyone can go to a burger restaurant on their special day, but how many children can celebrate on the Jolly Roger and walk the plank?

LOCATION, LOCATION, LOCATION

THINGS TO THINK ABOUT

How old is the birthday girl or boy? This may seem obvious to you the parent, but what you plan for a five year old can be seen as deeply un-cool for their eight-year-old sibling.

TODDLERS

For toddlers, of two or three, a party is more for your benefit as a get together with other parents or your immediate family or godparents. Activities are no more high brow than playing with balloons (not letting them touch the ground), bouncing balls, dancing to Ring o' Roses or playing with their favourite toys.

PRE-SCHOOL AGE

At four or five, most children will have a wider circle of friends as they start play school or proper school. Parties start to assume great importance in their hectic social whirl. Such parties are probably best at home where there will be plenty of distractions.

AGE SIX TO EIGHT

From about the age of six or seven, expect and encourage greater involvement from your child. These can be really fun years as children's imaginations go into overdrive. Their social skills also improve, so you can guarantee a couple of hours of high spirits and frenzied activity. Your home, garden or the local church/village hall are all ideal – having plenty of space at this age to burn off some energy (theirs, not yours) is vital.

NUMBERS

Much as little Molly would like to invite her entire class of thirty 'close' friends, think of your sanity and ability to act as a sheep dog. Manageable numbers are generally calculated as the age of the child plus one or two extras. When having a party for the under-threes, this rule can be disregarded as long as each toddler is accompanied by a parent. Bear in mind that if your themed party involves team games or make believe, you may need to increase the guest numbers accordingly to an easily divisible number, such as eight.

OLDER CHILDREN

From the age of nine or ten, it is really important to consider the child's likes and dislikes. At this age, activity-type parties out of doors or in another location (swimming pools or sports centres) can be a good option. Another alternative is to invite a small group of friends over for a 'girls-night-in' and a sleepover.

11

TIMING

Two to two-and-a-half hours is plenty for older children. Believe me! It is amazing what you can fit in to this length of time. Unlike adults, children don't need to 'warm up'. They are raring to go the moment they arrive. Any longer and the birthday boy or girl will be running on empty and tempers are likely to get frayed. Far better to go out on a high and leave the guests wanting more.

GOOD ICE BREAKER

SNAP! Using a packet of Snap playing cards, which are extremely cheap, hide half around the house and garden (some obvious, others more hidden) with a small wrapped sweet or chocolate coin attached to the back. Divide the other half amongst the guests as they arrive. Set them off looking for their matching pair.

SUGGESTED PARTY BREAKDOWN

It's useful to have a running order to ensure the party progresses smoothly and you avoid those 'what shall we do next' moments.

First 30 minutes
Guests arrive – have an immediate activity that they can all join in, such as decorating a plate or place card holder. If it's a costume party, have a dressing-up station and another adult on hand to act as wardrobe mistress.

Next 60 minutes
Structured games and play

Next 30 minutes
Birthday tea

Next 30 minutes
Quiet games, present opening and giving out of party bags

The other essential part of timing is to put a time limit on some activities and to alternate competitive and non-competitive games. Pass the Parcel for five to ten minutes is fun; stretch it to twenty and everyone will be getting fidgety. It is a far better idea to repeat an activity in another guise later. Try to arrange it so that everyone wins a small prize.

THE CAKE

The most important point about a birthday cake is a great design and presentation with a flourish. Not all party cakes require candles, and personally I think novelty candles (musical and re-lighting versions) are best avoided as they can make younger children over-excited or even upset them. It's far better to concentrate on the design of the cake and have simple coloured cake candles or tiny tapers stuck into cake holders.

Themed party cakes are simpler to make than you might think and if you are not keen on baking, decorate a shop-bought cake or barter with a friend who likes baking – do a swap with your skills. Try to cut the cake so that every child has a cake decoration or a piece of coloured icing. If you have two similar birthday cakes, one can be pre-cut and wrapped in advance, ready for the goody bags, to save time.

GOOD RELATIONS

Don't force grandparents to attend the party. Some will love to take part in the hustle and bustle. For others who are more elderly or less active, a more sedate family tea at another time would be a better option.

TIP

Always plan a couple of extra games or activities to keep up your sleeve in case they are required.

RECORDING THE DAY

Birthdays are one of the important rites of passage for children and it is great to share the day with relatives that cannot be there. Have one of the adult helpers or an older brother or sister in charge of the camera or video camera and take plenty of shots. Other good options for costume parties include a Polaroid or digital camera, so all the guests can take away a souvenir of the day with them.

AFTER THE EXCITEMENT

Keep a favourite video or two on standby, (nothing too action-packed) to put on at the end of the party in case you have any stragglers who are not collected on time by their parents. This helps your child to come down gently from their birthday-high and also means that you do not have to continue to amuse the children after an exhausting day.

GOODY BAGS AND PARTY MANNERS

Goody bags for guests to take away at the end of the party can be as eagerly awaited as the event itself. When you are having a themed birthday party, it is a great way to round off a memorable party.

GORGEOUS GOODY BAGS

When planned in advance, goody bags do not have to be expensive, even when catering for a large number of children. The trick is to hunt out bargain 'presents' over time and be inventive with the presentation. If you buy presents out of season or in sales, the cost can be halved.

To make the goody bags extra-special, think about the presentation. Bought party and gift bags can be expensive, but think of alternatives – purchase small paper carrier bags and customise with paint, stickers and stamps (this is something your child can do to help); sew up mini sacks from a double layer of crêpe paper; use two large squares of cellophane gathered up like a dolly bag (secure at the top with a rubber band and ribbon). There are loads more ideas within each theme.

Each bag should be labelled with the name of the child to whom it is being given. It is also a good idea to have a couple of spares (or at least spare contents) in case a disaster happens or a younger brother or sister tags along with a party guest.

GOODY BAG CONTENTS

Naturally, the contents will depend on the age group and the theme of the party, but small items with mass appeal include:

- Colourful pencils and pencil toppers
  - Key rings
  - Paints and brushes
- Craft materials
- Colouring books
- Joke and puzzle books
- Small puzzles
- Tiny toys
- Sweets/lollipops
- Mini photo frames
- Bubble blowers
- Funky pens and pencils
- Decks of cards
- Rubber stamps and stamp pads
- Transfers and stickers
  - Small torches
  - Balloons
  - Scrunchies and hair accessories
  - Toiletries and fun bath accessories
  - Beads and jewellery kits
  - Rubber reptiles and spiders

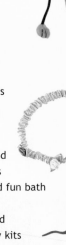

PARTY MANNERS

This is not an out-of-date guide to etiquette, but simply some common sense **pointers on polite behaviour for guests and hosts, so that the party is enjoyed by all** when everyone can be very over-excited.

GUESTS AND THEIR PARENTS

• Do reply to party invitations promptly.

• Remember to advise the host of any food allergies/pet allergies.

• If the party is a costume one, do dress up. You will feel left out if all the other guests are warring pirates, parrots and Long John Silvers and you are only wearing an eye patch.

• Remember to share games and activities and don't be upset if you are not a prize-winner.

• If there is some food you do not like, don't make a fuss. Simply eat what you like, but do try some new food – you may just like it!

• Say thank you when you leave.

• Do return to collect your child on time. After two hours of frenzied partying, the host will be fit to drop!

PARTY GIVER AND PARENTS

• Make sure you have assistance from helpers of your choice who will work! This sounds obvious, but unless you are firm with some parents who waft in with their child and offer to help, you'll find yourself organising the birthday party as well as racing around opening wine or making tea for the adults. Politely thank them and say you have plenty of help and little Fiona will be ready for collection at four.

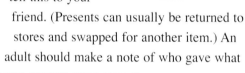

• Say thank you for your presents. If you already have the same book or game, do not tell this to your friend. (Presents can usually be returned to stores and swapped for another item.) An adult should make a note of who gave what as you unwrap your presents.

• Share your toys with the other children and take turns with games.

• If you have younger brothers and sisters, let them take part in the games and tea too.

• Write thank-you letters for your presents after the party.

PARTY CAKES

Now I know that some of you reading this will be saying things like 'I love the idea of cake decorating but I couldn't possibly do it myself!' Well, I promise that if you take a bit of time to read the instructions first and set aside a bit of time to make your creation, then you can!

The basic cake recipes are simple to follow and the sponge ones in particular are very easy. You just throw everything into a bowl and off you go! To save panic on the day before the party, you can always make the sponge in advance and freeze it (don't decorate it before freezing).

To clear up another confusing point, the ready-to-roll icing used in some of the recipes has a number of names. It's sometimes called fondant icing or sugarpaste. You can buy it ready-made from the supermarket or cake decorating shop or there's a recipe on page 21. It's easy to use – like edible modelling clay – but if you can't get hold of it or dislike the taste, you can always use marzipan or almond paste instead.

The only real secret behind successful cake decorating is having a go!

BASIC CAKE RECIPES

ALL-IN-ONE-SPONGE CAKE

This is a very easy recipe to use. You simply put all the ingredients in a bowl, mix them together and pour into a tin. It's as easy as using a cake mix!

1 Preheat the oven to 150°C/300°F/Gas mark 2. Then line your cake tin. Wipe a little butter or margarine around the inside of the tin using a piece of kitchen paper. Measure the circumference of the tin and cut a strip of greaseproof paper to that length and the height of the tin. Stand it upright around the inside of the tin. Place the tin on top of a sheet of greaseproof paper and draw round it. Cut out the shape and lay in the base of the tin.

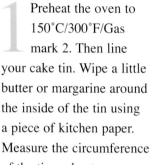

SQUARE TIN ROUND TIN	15cm (6in)	15cm (6in) 18cm (7in)	18cm (7in) 20cm (8in)	20cm (8in) 23cm (9in)
Self-raising flour	175g (6oz)	225g (8oz)	285g (10oz)	350g (12oz)
Caster sugar	115g (4oz)	175g (6oz)	225g (8oz)	285g (10oz)
Butter (softened)	115g (4oz)	175g (6oz)	225g (8oz)	285g (10oz)
Eggs (medium)	2	3	4	5
Milk	1 tbsp	1½ tbsp	2 tbsp	2 tbsp
Baking time (approx)	1 hr	1½ hrs	1½ hrs	1½–2 hrs

2 If you have a food mixer, sift the flour through a sieve into the mixing bowl and add the rest of the ingredients. Bind the mixture together on a slow speed. Then increase the speed of the mixer and beat for one minute until the mixture has turned pale and creamy. You can also use a hand-held electric mixer or simply beat the ingredients together using a wooden spoon.

3 Spoon into the prepared tin. Smooth the top and bake for the required time. When cooked the cake should be golden on top and pulling away slightly from the edges of the tin. If you stick a sharp knife or cake skewer into the middle, it should come out clean. Place a cooling rack over the cake tin and turn it upside down so the cake tips out on to the rack (you'll need to wear oven gloves). Carefully peel off the greaseproof paper and leave to cool.

When cooked and cooled, sponge cake can be frozen for up to three months.

PUDDING BOWL CAKE

The shape of this cake is ideal for the Horse on page 50 or the Mucky Pup on page 108

Use a 1-litre (2-pint) ovenproof pudding bowl and the amounts of cake mixture given for the three-egg mixture in the chart above. To prepare the bowl for baking, wipe some butter or margarine around the inside of the bowl using kitchen paper. Cut out a disc of greaseproof paper and lay this in the bottom of the bowl. Bake at 150°C/300°F/Gas mark 2 for about 1½ hours. When cooked, slide a palette knife around the edges of the cake to loosen it and turn out onto a cooling rack. Carefully peel the greaseproof disc off the base of the cake.

FAIRY CAKES

The amounts given for a three-egg mixture will make 12 fairy cakes. Spoon into paper cases and bake for 15-20 minutes at 180°C/350°F/Gas mark 4.

MIXING BOWL CAKE
This is used for the Dragon on page 64

Use a 2-litre (4-pint) ovenproof mixing bowl and the amounts given for a five-egg cake. Use the same instructions given for the pudding bowl to prepare the mixing bowl for baking.

LOAF TIN

For a 900-g (2-lb) loaf tin cake, grease the inside of the tin and lay a strip of greaseproof paper down the centre before baking. Use the amounts given for a three-egg mixture.

CHOCOLATE CAKE
and other tasty and colourful variations!

To make a chocolate cake, simply follow the same method and ingredients given for the all-in-one sponge cake (see previous page) but omit about a tablespoon of flour and replace it with a tablespoon of cocoa powder. Use more cocoa for a stronger colour and taste.

You can also stir a handful of chocolate chips or sugar strands (hundreds and thousands) into the mixture before baking to create a multi-coloured effect. Or give your cake a coloured or marbled effect by stirring a little food colour into the unbaked cake mixture. It's easy to alter the taste too. Add some grated lemon or orange zest, a few teaspoons of almond or coffee essence or even a couple of tablespoons of desiccated coconut.

FRUIT CAKE

Many people are frightened of making fruit cakes but they're really very simple to do. The added bonus of making your own, especially at Christmas, is that all the family can stir the mixture and make a wish and your home will smell wonderful as the cake cooks.

1 If you have left yourself enough time and are not reading this recipe late at night on Christmas Eve, place all the dried fruit into a bowl with the brandy. Cover it with a plate and leave to soak overnight. If you are reading this late at night on Christmas Eve, then all is not lost! Follow the recipe omitting the brandy and the soaking. You'll still end up with a tasty cake!

2 Preheat the oven to 150°C/300°F/Gas mark 2. To prepare the tin, line the inside of the tin as described in the all-in-one sponge cake recipe but use a double layer of greaseproof paper. Cut another two strips of greaseproof paper and stand these around the outside of the tin. Tie a length of string around the tin to hold them in place. This will prevent the edges of the cake from overcooking, so although a bit fiddly, it's worthwhile doing.

3 Cream the butter and sugar together in a large bowl. Beat in the eggs. Gently stir in the flour, spices and ground almonds. Add a spoonful more flour if the mixture looks runny.

4 Stir in the dried fruit, lemon zest and flaked almonds.

5 Spoon into the prepared tin and bake for 2-3 hours. To check if the cake is ready, stick a skewer or sharp, non-serrated knife in the middle. If it comes out clean, the cake is ready. Leave to cool in the tin.

	15cm (6in) ROUND FRUIT CAKE	20cm (8in) ROUND FRUIT CAKE
Currants	125g (4oz)	175g (6oz)
Sultanas	125g (4oz)	175g (6oz)
Raisins	125g (4oz)	175g (6oz)
Mixed peel	20g (^{3}/4oz)	45g (1^1/2oz)
Halved glacé cherries	45g (1^1/2oz)	75g (2^1/2oz)
Brandy (optional)	2-3 tbsp	4-5 tbsp
Butter	125g (4oz)	175g (6oz)
Brown sugar	125g (4oz)	175g (6oz)
Eggs	2 eggs	4 eggs
Plain flour	175g (6oz)	225g (8oz)
Mixed spice	^{1}/2 tsp	1 tsp
Cinnamon	^{1}/4 tsp	^{1}/2 tsp
Ground almonds	15g (^{1}/2oz)	30g (1oz)
Lemons (zest only)	^{1}/2	1
Flaked almonds	15g (^{1}/2oz)	30g (1oz)
Baking time (approx)	2–2^1/2 hrs	2^1/2–3 hrs

STORING A FRUIT CAKE

When the cake has cooled, turn it out of the tin but leave the greaseproof paper around the sides and base in place. Pierce the top a few times with a cocktail stick and spoon a couple of tablespoons of brandy over the top. Wrap the cake in two sheets of greaseproof and two sheets of tin foil. Store in a tin or cupboard, but not in a plastic container. The cake will keep for three months. You can feed it every week or so with more brandy if you wish.

ICING A FRUIT CAKE

Place the cake on the cake board and paint the top and sides with apricot jam using a pastry brush. Knead some marzipan until it's soft. Roll it out, lift and place over the top of the cake. Smooth the top first (to prevent air bubbles getting caught) and then the sides. Trim off any excess. Sprinkle the worksurface with icing sugar and knead and roll out some ready-to-roll icing. Lay it over the top of the cake, smooth down and trim.

GINGERBREAD

This is enough for one house or about twelve gingerbread people.

INGREDIENTS
250g (8oz) brown sugar
250g (8oz) white vegetable fat or butter
250g (8 fl oz) black treacle
1 egg (medium)
625g (1lb 6oz) plain flour
1 tsp bicarbonate of soda
2 tsp cinnamon
3 tsp ground ginger
1 tsp ground nutmeg

1 Mix the sugar and fat together in a large bowl. Add the treacle and egg and beat until smooth.

2 Sift all the dry ingredients together in another bowl then gradually mix these into the treacle mixture. It will become very stiff and you may need to use your hands. If you use a food mixer, then it's easy!

3 Divide the resulting ball of dough into quarters and wrap each quarter in cling film and place in the fridge for at least an hour.

4 Follow the instructions given in the gingerbread house recipe on page 80 for rolling and cutting out the dough.

The uncooked dough will keep wrapped in the fridge for up to three days.

BASIC ICING RECIPES

BUTTERCREAM

Makes 1 quantity

INGREDIENTS
250g (8oz) butter (softened)
500g (1lb 2oz) icing sugar
1–2 tbsp hot water

Place the ingredients into a mixing bowl and bind together using a food mixer on a slow speed. Increase the speed and beat until light and fluffy.

You can alter the flavour of the buttercream by adding a few drops of a flavoured essence such as vanilla, lemon or peppermint.

To make chocolate buttercream, mix a heaped tablespoon of cocoa with some hot water to make a paste then beat into the buttercream.

For coffee buttercream, mix two teaspoons of instant coffee with a teaspoon of hot water and add to the buttercream.

READY-TO-ROLL ICING

Also known as sugarpaste, fondant or rolled fondant icing, this is an easy-to-use and very versatile icing. It can be used to cover cakes and also for making models. It will harden when exposed to the air so keep any unused icing sealed in plastic bags until required.

You should be able to find this icing ready-made and sometimes ready-coloured in supermarkets or cake decorating shops (look up your nearest in the phone book) but here's a recipe just in case. Use home-made icing within a week.

INGREDIENTS
30ml (2 tbsp) liquid glucose
(available from chemists, supermarkets and cake decorating shops)
500g (1lb 2oz) icing sugar
1 egg white (or equivalent amount of dried egg white mixed with water)

Place the icing sugar in a bowl. Make a well in the centre. Pour the glucose and egg white into the well and stir using a wooden spoon.

Finish mixing everything together by hand. The icing should feel silky and smooth. Double wrap until required in two plastic food bags.

GLACE ICING

An easy-to-make icing that's useful for topping things like fairy cakes.

INGREDIENTS
250g (8oz) icing sugar
30ml (2 tbsp) water

Sift the icing sugar into a bowl and stir in the water. The icing should coat the back of a spoon. If it's too thick, add a few drops of extra water. If it seems too runny, stir in a little extra icing sugar.

Use a teaspoon to carefully spoon the icing onto the top of the cakes. To colour, stir in a couple of drops of liquid or paste food colour. For a tangy lemon alternative, use lemon juice instead of water.

ROYAL ICING

Because of the slight risk of food poisoning from using uncooked egg, I recommend you use one of the dried egg white products available from the supermarket or cake decorating shops. Read the instructions on the side of the packet in case they differ slightly from the ones given here.

If you want to use real eggs, use two egg whites in place of the dried egg white and water.

If you are making the royal icing to glue the gingerbread house together you can miss out the lemon and glycerine, but if, for example, it's for a **Christmas cake with peaks of royal** icing which looks like snow, you'll need to keep them in. The glycerine stops the icing from turning to concrete and you won't be able to get your knife through it otherwise!

INGREDIENTS
120ml (4fl oz) warm water
2 sachets (20g/ 3/4oz) dried egg white
1kg (2lb) icing sugar
15ml (1 tbsp) lemon juice
15ml (1 tbsp) glycerine

Reconstitute the egg white with the water as instructed on the packet. Whisk it until frothy. Stir in about a quarter of the sugar. Gradually add the rest of the sugar, lemon and glycerine until the mixture binds together. (Add extra water drop by drop if necessary.)

Beat the icing on a slow speed for five minutes until the icing stands up in peaks.

Place the icing into a plastic container with a tight fitting lid. Lay a strip of cling film directly on top of the icing and replace the lid until required. Stir before use.

MAKING A PIPING BAG

You can buy these ready-made from kitchen and cake decorating shops. You can also find plastic and metal syringe-type piping sets.

The advantages of making your own bags are they're inexpensive and you don't have any messy washing up to do afterwards!

1 To make two bags, cut a square of greaseproof paper off a roll and fold in half diagonally to form two triangles. Slide a knife along the fold to separate them.

2 Using one triangle, take corner 'C' and fold it round to line up with 'B'. The cone shape should form almost immediately.

3 Take corner 'A' and fold round the cone to line up with 'B' at the back . The point of the cone should be sharp.

4 Fold points 'A' and 'C' over a couple of times inside the top edge of the bag to secure it.

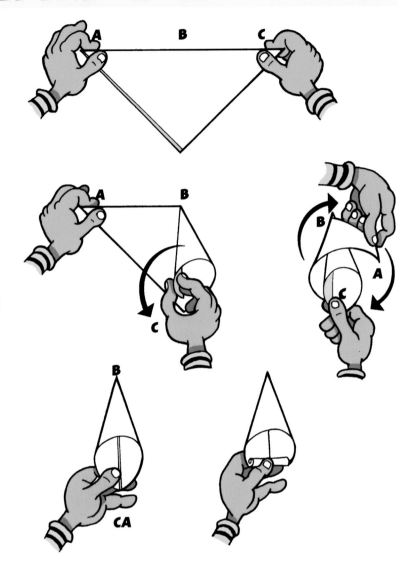

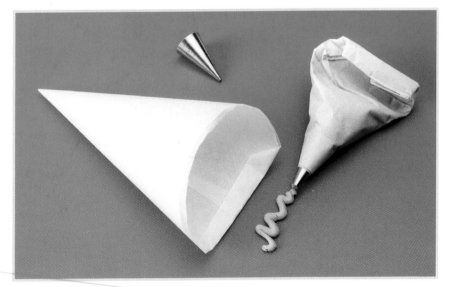

5 If using a piping nozzle, snip a tiny triangle off the end and drop the nozzle inside. Place some icing inside the bag and fold the open end over a few times to close the bag and force the icing out of the nozzle.

6 If you're not using a nozzle place the icing into the bag. Fold the end over a few times to close the bag and force the icing down to the point. Snip a tiny triangle off the end.

HINTS AND TIPS

FOOD COLOURS

The best colours to use are food pastes rather than liquids. Because they're thicker, they tend not to alter the consistency of the icing when mixed in. You can find them in supermarkets, cake decorating and kitchen shops. Knead it into ready-to-roll icing or marzipan and stir it into buttercream.

If you can only get hold of liquid colour, don't despair. It is useable but you may need to knead or mix in extra icing sugar to stop it becoming too runny.

CLEANING MARZIPAN AND READY-TO-ROLL ICING

If you've got a dusty icing sugar smudge mark ruining your creation, wipe it away with a soft, damp paintbrush when you've finished. The area may look shiny for a short while but it will revert to a matt finish eventually.

PREVENTING PROBLEM CRUMBS!

If you're covering your cake with buttercream, it's easy to get cake crumbs caught up in the icing which can ruin the appearance of the cake.

To prevent this happening, first spread a thin coating of buttercream over the outside of the cake. Then place the cake in the fridge. As the buttercream hardens it will 'glue' all those troublesome crumbs to the side of the cake. After an hour or so, you can take the cake out and spread a thicker layer of buttercream over the cake.

SOFTENING MARZIPAN

You can soften marzipan in the microwave by heating on high for about 15 seconds. Don't overdo it as the centre can get very hot and could cause a burn.

HANDY CAKE CUTTING HINT!

Your cakes will go much further if you slice them up into fingers rather than wedges.

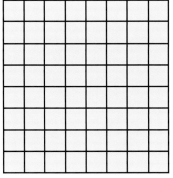

COLOURING COCONUT AND SUGAR

Colour coconut green and you've got instant grass. Colour it brown or black and you've got realistic gravel.

Place the coconut into a bowl. Add some food colour paste. Mix the colour into the coconut, preferably by hand as this is easiest. You can wear a disposable plastic glove to protect your hand from staining. Colour sugar using exactly the same method.

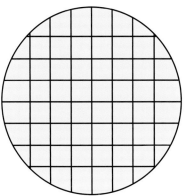

NUMBER CAKES

There are quite a few ways to make number cakes. The easiest way is to use a ready shaped cake tin. These can be bought or hired from cake decorating shops and some larger supermarkets.

However, by chopping up cakes, you can also make any number you like out of round and square baked cakes. Once you have assembled the cake, make sure that all the tops of all the various bits of cake are level before you buttercream them.

The cake and board sizes are suggestions only. Use bigger or smaller, depending upon how many people are coming to the party!

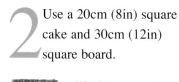

2 Use a 20cm (8in) square cake and 30cm (12in) square board.

1 Use a 15cm (6in) square cake and 25cm (10in) square board or 20cm (8in) cake and 30cm (12in) board. Place diagonally on board.

TIP
If you're wary about cutting straight into cake, make a square or disc of greaseproof paper the same size as the cake and cut that up first. Use the cut pieces as templates.

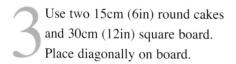 Use two 15cm (6in) round cakes and 30cm (12in) square board. Place diagonally on board.

Use a 20cm (8in) square cake and 30cm (12in) square board.

MAKING THE NUMBER 4 CAKE

First cut your square cake to shape (see how to do this using the guide above right) and slice it in half.

Carefully reassemble the cake, filling the middle with buttercream. Spread more buttercream around the top and sides.

See tip on page 23 on how to prevent cake crumbs mixing with the buttercream on the outside of the cake and spoiling your creation. Decorate with colourful sweets. Details of how to make the fairies used to decorate the cake in the photo can be found on page 70.

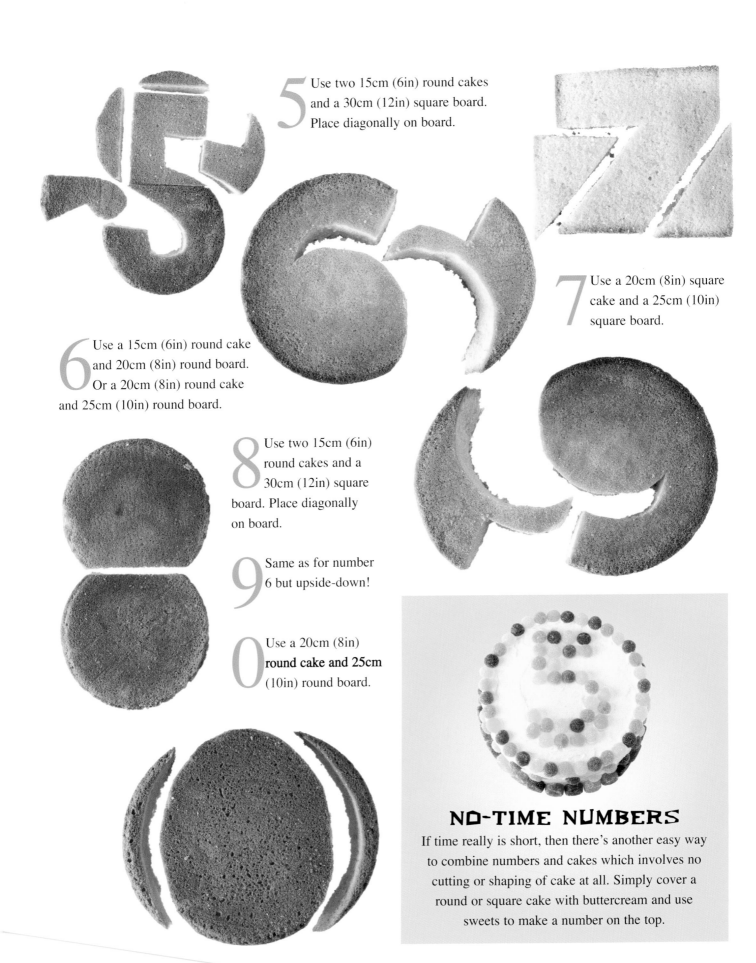

5 Use two 15cm (6in) round cakes and a 30cm (12in) square board. Place diagonally on board.

6 Use a 15cm (6in) round cake and 20cm (8in) round board. Or a 20cm (8in) round cake and 25cm (10in) round board.

7 Use a 20cm (8in) square cake and a 25cm (10in) square board.

8 Use two 15cm (6in) round cakes and a 30cm (12in) square board. Place diagonally on board.

9 Same as for number 6 but upside-down!

0 Use a 20cm (8in) **round cake and 25cm** (10in) round board.

NO-TIME NUMBERS

If time really is short, then there's another easy way to combine numbers and cakes which involves no cutting or shaping of cake at all. Simply cover a round or square cake with buttercream and use sweets to make a number on the top.

HOLES

It can be fiddly to cut holes out of cakes so the easiest way to make numbers with holes in (4, 6, 8, 9, 0) is to ignore the hole completely and to place some sort of decoration over the space where the hole would be to hide it. The fairies do this on the number 4 cake.

BLACK HOLES!

Another easy way to make holes is to fake them! First buttercream the cake as usual, then place a flat disc (or a triangle if it's a number 4) of black coloured ready-to-roll icing or marzipan on top of the cake to represent the hole. Then decorate as usual.

REAL HOLES

If you want to make a real hole as on the number 8 football cake it's still fairly simple – see the instructions on the right.

MAKING THE NUMBER 8 CAKE

First, cut your cakes to shape and slice both cakes in half. Cut holes out of the top slices only.

Colour a little buttercream black and the rest green.

Spread the black on the base cake where it will be visible through the holes in the top layer. Don't go right to the edges or the black might ooze out of the sides and mess up the green on the outside of the cake. Spread green buttercream over the rest of the base and around the sides of the holes in the top piece.

Reassemble the cake and carefully spread buttercream over the top and sides and decorate with footballers. Add a little green coloured coconut if you wish. Details of how to do this are on page 23.

Party Themes

From pirates to princesses and cowboys to explorers – here's a party theme to delight every birthday boy and girl

CHOOSING A THEME

Choosing a theme is a great way to make any party go with a swing and to give yourself a head start with planning.

Any parent will know what the current dressing-up obsession is with their child and their favourite story themes. Costume parties are the ultimate fantasy for a would-be pirate king or pre-Raphaelite princess. Plus they are great fun for all ages and can encourage unstructured play without the need for constant games or activities. Adult helpers will also enjoy entering into the party spirit and demonstrating their amateur dramatic skills once they are in character!

The following pages show themes which are suitable for both sexes. However, there is no limit to your imagination – my only advice is, make it easy to interpret into costumes and props. For example, most parents can rustle up a Wild West outfit for little Harry at the drop of a stetson, but dressing up as the Eiffel Tower could demand more time and ingenuity than you may have available!

Discuss with the birthday boy or girl their favourite ideas. Rather than giving them an open choice, perhaps make a shortlist of three from which they can choose. Whatever theme you decide on, you will need to consider costumes, how to set the scene (the 'theatre') with decorations and props, invitations and goody bags. This needs lateral thinking and perhaps a glass of wine to help the ideas flow. A good starting point is to look at children's books. The illustrations are sure to spark off several ideas. Keep making notes over a few days, before you decide on the final plan.

PIRATE PARTY

This is a party with plenty of potential and is bound to go down in party folklore in your neighbourhood. Costumes are a breeze to make or adapt from everyday clothes and you can transform your home and garden into a Jolly Roger at the drop of a parrot.

'SHIVER ME TIMBERS'
INVITATIONS

There are many options depending on your creative skills. A good idea for many home made invitations is to use folded 'blank' cards available in packs from art and craft shops. Decorate the front and write the party details inside or print out from a computer to save time.

Ideas include a skull and crossbones, paper flags, big canvas knot stuck on 'sailcloth' (calico), illustration by the birthday girl or boy. The invitation can be written as shown here.

Ahoy – me hearties

Cap'n Jack and his trusty crew are sailing into port on 20 July to celebrate his 8th Birthday. Calling all land lubbers to enjoy some swash-buckling fun at his Pirate Party from 4-6.

RSVP
Cap'n Jack
c/o The Jolly Roger
Address
Telephone number

Prizes of booty for the jolliest or most fearsome costumes.

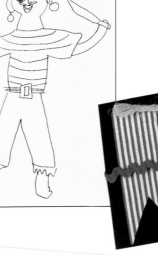

COSTUMES

• Wear baggy trousers or shorts in plain colours. If they are old, cut off the bottoms with a zigzag edge.

• Stripy T-shirts with white and black, red or blue stripes are ideal. Paint your own pirate shirt T-shirt with fabric paint (use masking tape to define the stripes and stuff the shirt with paper to prevent the paint soaking through to the other side).

• Heavy leather belts or more fabric tied in a sash around the waist.

• Make a cardboard cutlass and colour it with poster paint.

• Use large brass curtain rings, looped with thread as instant earrings to loop over the ears.

• Make a newspaper hat for the pirate or make a hat from black art paper with a skull and crossbones stuck on (see folding instructions on page 127).

• Black eye patches.

• Every pirate should wear a bandanna tied around their head. These can be cheap to buy in markets or bargain shops. Alternatively, buy some plain red fabric or gingham and cut into 50cm (20in) squares.

'AHOY - ME HEARTIES'

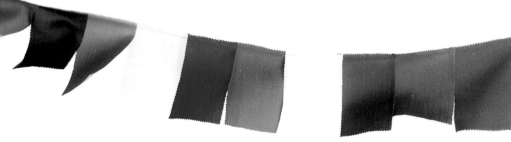

SETTING THE SCENE

TREASURE CHEST

Any toy chest can be turned into a treasure chest. (Disguise if necessary by painting or by wrapping in brown or gold crêpe paper.) Prop it open and bulk out with a blanket. Cover the top with more crêpe or tissue paper. Drape old jewellery over, or place chocolate coins and any other booty, such as sports trophies (real or plastic), compasses, friendship bracelets, at the top.

NAUTICAL BUNTING

Make nautical bunting from coloured paper or scraps of fabric and sew or staple onto seam binding. Pin to the washing line or festoon around the house.

PIRATE FLAG

Using some plain black fabric, cut out a rectangle for a flag at least 30cm x 45cm, (12in x 18in) stick on a felt skull and crossbones, or use a fusible web (such as Bondaweb) to iron on one in white fabric. Attach to a bamboo pole and drive into the ground. If you make several, plant one near the front gate.
See template on page 127.

PIRATE PLACE SETTINGS

• Use a plain coloured oil cloth or white paper table cloth with a big red cross made of crêpe paper or fabric.
• Make place mats from coloured paper with circles, squares or triangles to look like nautical flags.
• Have plain or stripy red or black napkins. Place cards can have names such Pirate Nimble Nancy or Pirate Slippery Sam.

Outdoor Fun

• Set up a hammock if possible.
• Make an awning from some calico or an old sheet. Tie each corner to four sturdy poles and make guy ropes to keep the poles vertical. (Use tent poles and guys if you already have them.) You can either set up the birthday tea table underneath or put down some blankets and cushions and have a swash-buckling pirate story-telling session.

GAMES AND ACTIVITIES

• **Sack race.** See page 40.

• **3-legged Long John Silver race.**

• **Make pirate hats** from newspaper against the clock. Give a quick demonstration and then let each guest make up their own (see template on page 127).

• **Treasure hunt** – give the guests clues or a map leading them around the garden to points with signs such as Cannibal Cove, Pegleg Point, Crocodile Swamp. At the final point, have one big prize for the winner and consolation prizes (chocolate coins) for the runners up.

• **Pin the Beak on the Parrot** (variation of Pin the Tail on the Donkey).

• **Make a telescope.** Before the party save toilet rolls or kitchen rolls (get friends and neighbours to help with this!). Cover one end with coloured cellophane. Stick down or secure with a rubber band. Cover with a piece of white paper and get the children to decorate with coloured pens. This is a good game to quieten things down or to use as an opener as guests arrive.

• **Losers to competitive games** can choose to walk the plank or take a booby prize such as lemon drops or other eek-inducing sweets. For the plank, balance a narrow plank above a paddling pool and blind fold the victim. Turn them around a couple of times before getting them to walk to the other side. Have towels on standby! If you have a slide, place the pool at the bottom. This type of activity must be supervised by an adult or two.

• **Throw the Rats Overboard** – Make up rats from old grey socks filled with rice or lentils and fastened with rubber bands. Have a tail of wool hanging out the end and stick on wobbly eyes. See how far the children can throw them.

Goody bags

• Cut up a black bin liner and resew or tape into smaller goody sacks. Stick on a photocopied skull and crossbones. Tie at the top with some coloured ribbon or fabric.

• Cut cream calico into squares (like sails) and knot at the top with thick string or thin rope.

• Ideas for contents: plastic jewellery plundered from the treasure chest, silver or gold chocolate coins, oranges (to prevent scurvy on long sea voyages), glass bottles of cola relabelled 'Best Navy Rum', any of the props they may have been given when dressing up.

PIRATE SHIP

Ahoy there! Anyone for a piece of cake and a few chocolate coins, me hearties?

INGREDIENTS
Mixing bowl cake
(see page 18)
2 quantities chocolate buttercream
(see page 20)
1 quantity plain, uncoloured buttercream
2 x 144g (5oz) boxes chocolate sticks
(see TIP box below)
Breadsticks
Rice paper
Black food colour pen
Blue food colour
Chocolate coins

EQUIPMENT
Carving knife
Palette knife
30cm (12in) round cake board
3 sandwich flags (available from
kitchen equipment shops)
Scissors

1 Carve the cake into a boat-like shape. Slice it in half horizontally once or twice and fill with chocolate buttercream. Place it in position on the cake board. Spread chocolate buttercream around the top and sides.

3 To make the masts, carefully stick a sandwich flag into a breadstick. (This might take two or three goes!) Put the one with the flag in the centre. Snap a little off the other two breadsticks to make them shorter and place them behind and in front of the central mast.

2 Carefully press the chocolate sticks around the sides of the ship. Break them if necessary to follow the contours of the ship. The top sticks should be higher than the deck of the ship so that the coins don't fall off later.

TIP
You can leave out the chocolate sticks if you wish. Your pirate ship will still look impressive!

PIRATE SHIP

4 Cut out three rice paper rectangles for sails and trace over the skull and crossbones design using a black food colour pen.

5 Stick a sail to each mast using a little plain buttercream. Partially mix a little blue food colour into the rest of the plain buttercream and swirl it around the cake board to look like a choppy sea.

6 Stick the other two sandwich flags towards the back of the cake and fill the pirate ship with chocolate coins.

SPORTY PARTY

'WE ARE THE CHAMPIONS!'

A sports-themed party is ideal for energetic youngsters and will encourage them to burn off some of their never-ending energy. This party theme is ideal for older children, of eight years plus, where they can be actively involved with the planning of activities and decorations.

INVITATIONS

If you have a football-mad child, make card invitations in the shape of a football strip (use coloured card to copy their favourite team). Make a template to trace around. Your child's age can be written or stuck on like a player's number.

Or make invitations in the shape of a rugby or tennis ball, football trophy or swimming costume (add stickers for a spotty costume). As this will be an activity-based party, it is a good idea for guests to wear shorts, T-shirts and trainers, so mention this on the invitation.

BE A GOOD SPORT

All sporting champions
are invited to
David's 9th
Birthday Party
at the sports centre in
(town name)
on 10th September at 2.30
followed by an Olympic feast at home.

RSVP
David Hat-Trick Smith
Address
Telephone number

Wear shorts and trainers/Bring a
swimming costume and towel
(or whatever is appropriate)

SETTING THE SCENE

The simplest option if you have a local sports centre or swimming pool, is to use this as the party venue. Many now hire out pools or pitches for birthdays, with a choice of various activities such as circuit training or indoor soccer.

Make sure you discuss the choice of sports with the birthday child – they will, of course, want to play their favourites! It may be easier to hire a mini-bus to transport all the partygoers to and from your home, so that guests don't go astray looking for the party venue.

Other more unusual options include a bowling alley or ice skating rink. If this is not an option because of distance or cost – do not despair – your home can easily be converted into an Olympic stadium at minimal effort and expense.

GAMES AND ACTIVITIES

As prizes for games, why not make some quick winners' rosettes out of gathered strips of crêpe paper stuck behind a circle of card? Try to ensure that each child receives a rosette during the party.

FOURTH DIVISION

A great icebreaker as guests arrive, prepare four-part 'jigsaws' of famous sports personalities (use photographs from newspapers or magazines). Try to use similar sizes of images, or photocopy to a similar size. Cut into four. Randomly hand out four parts of different puzzles to each child. The children have to circulate quickly and swap parts. The first to make a whole picture is the winner. Give each guest an extra point for the name of the sportsman or woman.

GOAL!

This is very active, indoors or out! It can be played in heats to find an eventual winner. Give two balloons to each player – one round and one long. The round balloons should be different colours so they do not get confused. Each player uses the long balloon as a bat and tries to dribble or hit the round balloon into the goal (a cardboard box or laundry basket) at the far end of the room. The first to score a goal is the winner of that heat.

Goody Bags

Why not try to imitate sports bags with drawstring bags sewn from brightly coloured rip stop nylon or jersey (or look for cheap pencil cases)? Fill with high-energy drinks or snack bars, fruit juices and shoe laces, skipping ropes, chalk for hopscotch, sports stickers or swap cards. Check sports shops for other pocket money ideas.

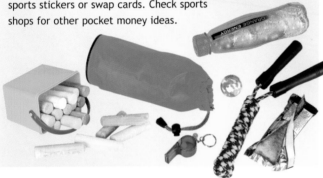

MATCH TIE

A picture game in which flash cards of equipment (football, golf club) have to be matched up to the sport. Cut out pictures from sports magazines or download pictures from the Internet or clip art software. Try to include some more unusual sports for older children. To make this more active, children can sit in a line with the names of the sports laid around the room/garden or pinned on the washing line, for the children to grab.

SACK RACE

Some of the most traditional games are still the best. Get some hessian sacks from a local greengrocer or farmer, or sew some sacks using fabric from the remnant bin of a fabric or furnishing store. Depending on how many sacks are available and the number of party guests, the races can be run in heats or as a relay race with children hopping to a fixed point and then swapping with a team mate.

FANTASY FOOTBALL AND DESIGN-A-JOCKEY

Design a new football strip for your fantasy team or racing silks for your own stable. Photocopy and enlarge the drawings shown below and get children to colour in patterns and colours of their choice. Have plenty of inexpensive colouring pens on hand. Buy packs of coloured sticky stars and spots from stationers for the racing silks. Give a prize for the most outlandish outfit.

CIPHER SPORTS

A good game for cooling down before food or going home. Encode the attached list for each guest. Each code unravels to spell out a sport (or sports personality). To encode the words, or to make up more suggestions, remove vowels, make alternative letters jump by one letter, or turn into anagrams.

cricket
rowing
football
tiddlywinks
cross country
skiing
tennis
horse racing
speedway
lacrosse
ice hockey

salsa dancing
rugby union
down hill
bobsleigh
formula 1 racing
basketball
curling
ping pong
athletics
swimming
badminton

Answers: golf, skiing, rowing

The children have to work out and write down the correct names. Explain the code breaking methods to the children before they start. For example, badminton becomes bdmntn (vowels removed), lacrosse becomes madrpste (jumping alternative letters), football becomes float lob (anagram).

Other activity ideas

For younger children, bouncy castles are a guaranteed winner, or you can set up your own circuit training at home and in the garden with skipping, ping pong, hopscotch, table football or archery. Each guest has a set amount of time at each activity with umpires keeping scores for each sport.

FOOTBALL CRAZY

On this cunning design, the footballer is traced onto rice paper using a food colour pen. He's then cut out and stuck onto the cake. Not only is it a quick and easy way to put a picture on a cake but it's all edible too!

INGREDIENTS
1 sheet rice paper
Black food colour pen for outline (available from kitchen equipment or cake decorating shops)
Assorted coloured food colour pens (optional – only needed if you want to colour in the design)
15cm (6in) round sponge cake
(see page 17)
1 quantity green-coloured buttercream
(see page 20)
Football-shaped sweets

EQUIPMENT
Scissors
20cm (8in) round cake board
Carving knife
Palette knife
Fork

Tip
Can't find any football sweets? Use balls of ready-to-roll icing or marzipan instead!

1 Trace over the outline of the footballer on this page using a black food colour pen and a sheet of rice paper. Colour sections if you wish and draw the recipient's age on the jersey.

2 Carefully cut out the figure and place to one side.

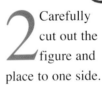

42

4 Place the figure on top of the cake. Stick one football sweet on the top of the cake and the rest around the base.

3 Split the cake in half horizontally and fill the middle with buttercream. Reassemble the cake and spread a thick layer over the outside of the cake. Use a fork to give it a grassy effect.

SACK RACE

If you have time, (and lots of people coming to the party), you could make two or three of these cakes and have them racing across the tea table!

INGREDIENTS
Pudding bowl cake (see page 17)
1 quantity buttercream (see page 20)
75g (3oz) red coloured ready-to-roll icing (see page 21)
75g (3oz) flesh-coloured ready-to-roll icing*
Black food colour (see TIP box)
700g (1lb 9oz) brown coloured ready-to-roll icing*
Icing sugar
Green food colour

Use either 'paprika' food colour paste or a mixture of yellow and pink food colour to make a skin tone similar to the one in the picture. For darker tones, use chestnut or brown food colour pastes.

EQUIPMENT
Carving knife
Palette knife
20cm (8in) round cake board
Small paintbrush
Rolling pin
Small sharp knife
Piping bag (see page 22)

1 Stand the cake so that its widest part forms its base. Split it horizontally once or twice and fill with buttercream. Place in position on the cake board and spread buttercream around the top and sides.

2 To make the figure, first roll the red icing into a ball. Squash the ball slightly to make a flattish base ready for the head and place on top of the cake. Roll about 50g (2oz) of the flesh coloured icing into a ball for her head. Roll the leftover flesh-coloured sugarpaste into two small sausage shapes for arms.

3 Stick the head on top of the body using a dab of water. Paint eyes and mouth onto the face using black food colour and a fine paintbrush.

TIP
If you don't want to paint, use a food colour pen to make dots for eyes and a piping nozzle to make a smiley mouth. (See Waterbabies cake on page 92)

4 Knead the brown icing until pliable. Dust your worksurface with icing sugar and roll it out. Cut out a rectangle about 40cm x 15cm (16in x 6in). Roll the icing up like a bandage and, holding it vertically, unroll it around the cake. (There is a picture showing how to do this in the 'Bag of Sweets' instructions on page 106.)

5 Trim and neaten the join and the base. Stick the arms onto the body with dabs of water and bend them over the sides of the sack.

6 Place a little buttercream into a piping bag and pipe squiggly hair onto the head. Add a tiny ball of red ready-to-roll icing as a hairband if you wish.

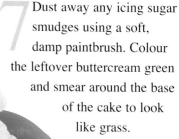

7 Dust away any icing sugar smudges using a soft, damp paintbrush. Colour the leftover buttercream green and smear around the base of the cake to look like grass.

Decorating Variation

This easy-to-make version involved taking the legs off a doll! Tie a piece of ribbon around the top of her body to preserve her modesty and insert her into the top of the sack.

WILD WILD WEST PARTY

'HOWDY PARDNER'

For a birthday party at home on the range, a Wild West theme with sheriffs, Native Americans plus law-dodging cowboys and cowgirls is guaranteed to raise the roof of any domestic saloon. So for a hoedown with plenty of yee-hah, read on!

INVITATIONS

Stick a feather or length of fringed felt on the card, draw a cactus, a sheriff's badge or a teepee and write as follows:

Lone Ranger Richard wants to round up all Ranch Hands for a Wild West Party.

Calling all Cowgirls and Boys, Squaws and Big Chiefs to the Birthday Reservation on 10 August from 2 to 4.30.

RSVP in writing or by smoke signals to:
Lone Ranger Richard
C/o The OK Corral
Address
Telephone number

COSTUMES

It's so simple to ride into the OK Corral – jeans, sturdy belts and checked shirts or sweat shirts are all that's needed from the cupboard, with the addition of a toy-store stetson and a bandanna (re-use a plaid napkin) tied around the neck. Alternatively fringe a 40cm (16in) square of checked fabric. Have some spares for guests.

If you are feeling adventurous, make a fringed 'leather' waistcoat from some brown felt or some chaps from some fake fur fabric tied around the waist. Make a sheriff's badge from gold card.

SETTING THE SCENE

• Use some bean poles lashed together and covered in a three-quarters-circle of calico as a instant teepee. Include props such as leather boots, coils of rope, denim jackets and perhaps even a bale of straw!

• Make 3D cacti from large painted cardboard boxes obtained from furniture or electrical stores. Paint them, then glue on pom poms to look like cactus flowers.

• Have check blankets or Aztec-type rugs dotted around.

GAMES

'YEE-HAA!'

- Have a pow-wow, sitting in a circle with a story.
- Lasso the cow (variation on hoopla). Have various soft toys dotted about the grass. Each contestant has to try to lasso one with a looped rope. Alternatively, in a confined space, use a stetson instead of a lasso.
- Beading, beadloom weaving or making friendships bracelets.
- Archery competition.
- Make a feather head-dress.
- Make a bead and seed picture. Using child-safe glue on a card background, use lentils and seeds to create a simple picture.
- Winners of games can be given a sheriff's badge cut from gold card.
- Organise a barn dance with country music and square dancing.
- Paint a totem pole. Photocopy an outline onto A3 paper for the guests to colour in (this is a good opener for when guests arrive – see below).

HOME ON THE RANGE

Terrific totem

Totem poles are created by Native Americans and include commemorative carved images of notable people, plus animals and birds with which the community felt a particular allegiance. Make your own using a cardboard tube, about 12cm (5in) in diameter and 1.8m tall (carpet stores will give these tubes away for free).

Paint with poster paint and add a curling snake detail. The Big Chief Thunderbird, eagle and wild bear are all cut from cardboard boxes, using the templates on page 128 and painted. Cut a slot in the top of the pole for the totem head to slide into. Stick an extra rectangle of card with four notches cut out, to the reverse of the eagle and bear motifs. Loop an elastic band around two notches, position at the right height on the totem and loop the band around the remaining notches.

RANCH FOOD FOR HUNGRY COWHANDS

Whether you are eating indoors or outdoors, make the meal seem like a picnic. Sit on old tree stumps or old cushions around a bonfire if outside. Suspend lanterns from punched tin cans from the trees at dusk. Indoors, keep it simple by covering the table in a white sheet decorated with black fabric paint to look like a cow hide. Food should be hearty and simple – bangers from a barbecue, baked potatoes and baked beans. Serve on paper plates with checkered napkins, or use enamel plates and swig 'moonshine' from enamel mugs (available from camping stores). Once washed, these can go into the goody bags.

TIP
Many children prefer savoury to sweet food. The birthday cake can be the sweet element and can always be cut up and put in the goody bag after a filling barbecue. However, remember the lighting of the candles and singing 'Happy Birthday' is essential, even for rough-tough cowhands.

GOODY BAGS

• Why not cut up old denim jeans (or buy for a song from charity shops) and whizz up into pouches using a sewing machine?

• Use cheap bandannas knotted as a swag bag. The scarf is then a major part of the goody bag

• Use mock suede or chamois leathers to make bag fringes and attach to more conventional brown paper bags.

• Contents: water pistols, friendship bracelets, beads, feathers and a length of leather cord to make Native American-style jewellery.

I'M A LITTLE HORSE

EQUIPMENT
25cm (10in) round
cake board
Carving knife
Palette knife
Rolling pin
Small sharp knife
Paintbrush

I'm a little horse, delicious of course.
You'll be shouting with force
for more than one...slice.
Hmmm...perhaps I should forget poetry
and keep to the cake decorating!

INGREDIENTS
Pudding bowl cake (see page 17)
1 quantity chocolate buttercream (see page 20)
500g (1lb 2oz) brown-coloured marzipan
(To make it brown, knead in either 6 teaspoons
of cocoa powder or some brown food colour
to create the desired shade)
Icing sugar for rolling out on
Bootlace sweets or similar
50g (2oz) green-coloured sugar or coconut
(see page 23)

1 Sit the cake on its widest part on the cake board. Split it horizontally two or three times and sandwich it back together with buttercream. Spread a thick coating of buttercream around the outside of the cake.

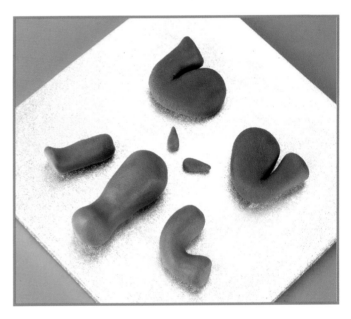

2 To make the girth, roll about 25g (1oz) marzipan into a sausage about 25cm (10in) long. Roll over it with a rolling pin to flatten and cut out a thin strip about 1.5cm (^{3}/4in) wide. Lay this over the horse's back.

3 Make saddle flaps by rolling about 45g (1^1/2oz) marzipan into a sausage shape. Squash it into an oval and cut in half. Stick one half either side of the horse. Make a second 45g (1^1/2oz) oval shape for the seat and stick on top of saddle flaps.

4 To make a back leg, roll 90g (3oz) into a sausage shape. Squash one end slightly to make a rounded thigh and slice a little off the other end to make a hoof. Bend in half and stick in position with the hoof pointing backwards. Repeat for the other back leg.

TIP
You can soften marzipan by placing it in the microwave and heating on full power for 15-20 seconds. Do not over-do it or the oils in the centre will get very hot and may cause a burn.

5 Make the nearest front leg using 60g (2oz) of marzipan. Roll it into a sausage. Slice a little off one end to make a hoof. Bend slightly and stick in position. Repeat using 30g (1oz) for the other leg which is straight and shorter. Position this one sticking straight out behind the head.

6 Make two tiny triangle shapes for the horse's ears and press a slight hollow into each one using the end of a paintbrush. Roll the remaining marzipan into a tapering oval shape for the horse's head. Stick it in position and press the edge of a sharp knife into the marzipan to make a line for his mouth. Poke two holes with the end of a paintbrush for nostrils.

7 Use strips of bootlace for the horse's mane and tail. Use shorter lengths for his fringe and longer for the tail. The buttercream on the cake should hold the laces on his neck and rear in place. You might need to use dabs of water on his head. Use buttercream if you need something stronger. Stick the ears in place using water or buttercream.

8 To finish, moisten the cake board with a little water and spoon the coloured sugar 'grass' around the horse. Alternatively, spread leftover buttercream on the board and sprinkle with coloured coconut.

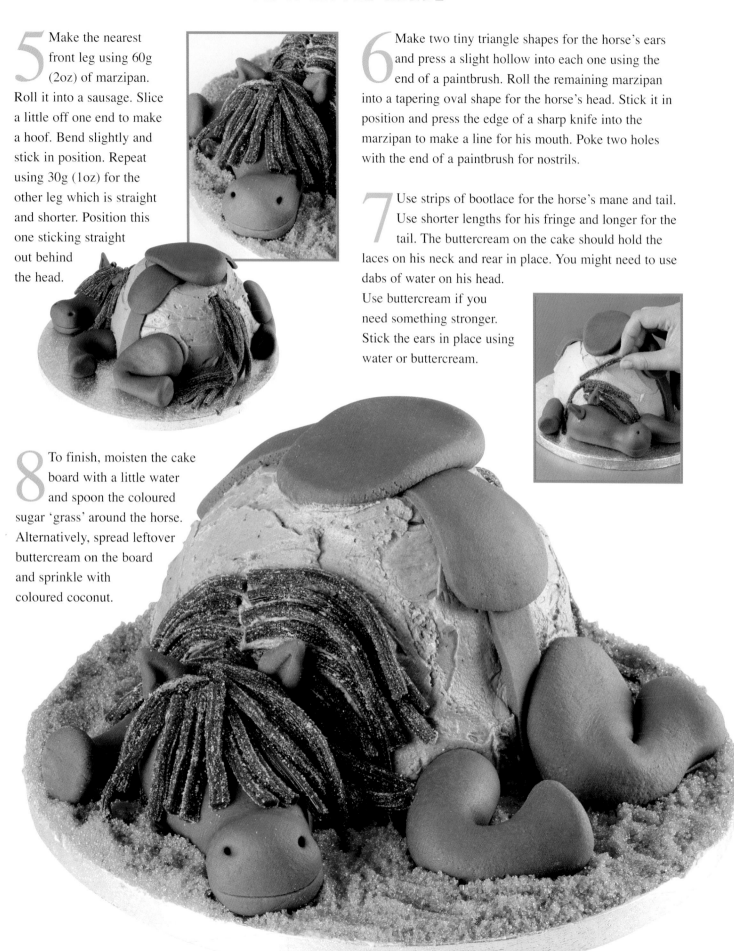

WILD WEST FORT

Will you help the cowboys bravely defend their stash of sweets against the sweet-toothed Native Americans or will you try to pinch the treasure too?

INGREDIENTS
18cm (7in) square cake
(see page 17)
1 quantity chocolate buttercream
(see page 20)
1/2 quantity green-coloured buttercream
2 boxes milk chocolate fingers
10 white chocolate fingers
Assorted sweets

EQUIPMENT
Carving knife
Palette knife
25cm (10in) square cake board
Fork
Sandwich flags
Native American
and Cowboy models

1 Level the top of the cake to make it flat. Split the cake once or twice horizontally and fill it with buttercream. Place the cake onto the cake board and spread buttercream around the sides and top.

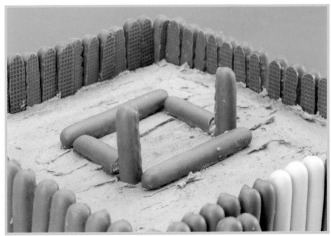

2 Press the chocolate fingers vertically around the sides of the cake. Use three white ones to make a door at the front.

3 To make the lookout post on top of the cake, lay two fingers flat on the top of the cake to form the front and back. Cut six fingers in half. To make one side wall, stand one half-finger upright and one half-finger on the cake surface. Repeat on the other side.

4 Using buttercream as glue, stick one more full-length finger at the front and four piled up at the back. Make up the two sides using piles of four half-fingers. Stick a final full-length finger across the front of the lookout post to form a window.

5 Make the roof by sticking seven white chocolate fingers horizontally across the top of the lookout post.

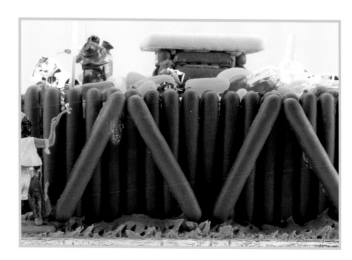

6 Stick any leftover fingers in upside-down 'V' formations around the sides of the cake with dabs of buttercream.

7 Spread the green buttercream around the cakeboard and use a fork to rough it up slightly to resemble grass.

8 Place the models in position. Stick the sandwich flags in place and fill the top of the fort with sweets.

TIP
If you're going to put a cowboy inside the hut, place him in position before you put the roof on!

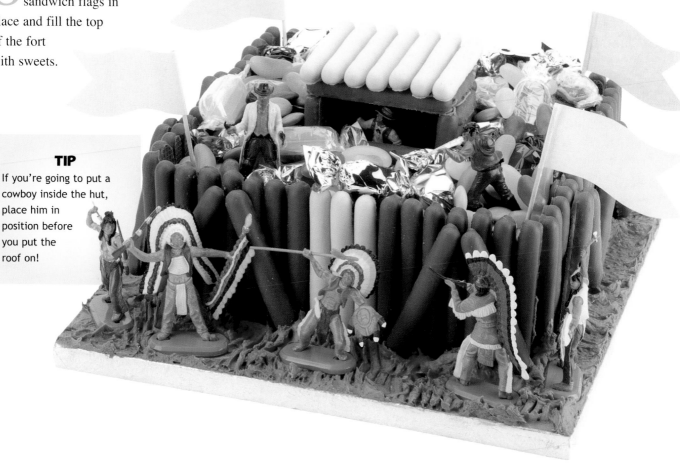

GREAT EXPLORERS' PARTY

For energetic children of all ages, an explorers' party is bound to appeal to their sense of adventure and is a brilliant excuse to have the party out-of-doors. Ask guests to wear jeans, shorts or old clothes.

INVITATIONS

Cut up some old maps and stick to cards. Randomly mark a big red X on the cards and draw the points of a compass. Or stick leaves onto a card with the party details.

DR LIVINGSTONE PRESUMES YOU WOULD LIKE TO COME TO A PARTY TO CELEBRATE LUCY'S 10TH BIRTHDAY. THE GREAT ADVENTURE TAKES PLACE ON 23RD AUGUST AT 4PM IN THE SWAMPS AND TROPICAL RAINFORESTS OF HER GARDEN. DARING EXPLORERS CAN BRING A SLEEPING BAG AND SLEEP OUT UNDER THE STARS.

RSVP: LUCY LIVINGSTONE
ADDRESS
TELEPHONE
MAP ATTACHED SO YOU CAN FIND THE WAY!

SETTING THE SCENE

This is really an outdoor party, so is ideal for summer holidays. Remember your garden is no longer a lawn and flower beds, but an exciting adventure playground in which children can let off steam and use up energy!

• Set up various tents dotted around the lawn – use instant pop-out tents, pup tents and old sheets or blankets slung over clothes horses or washing lines.
• Firmly tie two lines of stout rope, one above the other between two trees, so that kids can walk across.
• Use a sturdy kitchen table (not a trestle table) as a look-out post. Drive long bean poles into the ground at each corner and lash together with bunting or throw a camouflage net (or old net curtain dyed or painted) over the top.

• Put on a tape or CD of jungle music or wildlife noises. Hide the CD player under bushes.
• Make signs saying CAUTION! WILD BEARS, DO NOT FEED THE TIGERS and DO NOT WORRY THE SHEEP. Prop soft toys next to the signs.

GAMES AND ACTIVITIES

Many of the activities involve unstructured play, which allows adults some respite.

ADVENTURER

Tie ropes with a knot onto strong branches as improvised swings. To add some excitement, have a jumping off point, a paddling pool in the centre and landing 'mat' on the other side. Be prepared for wet clothes as some children inevitably jump in!

SCAVENGER HUNT

First split the children up into small teams. Provide a series of numbered written clues or directions leading to crossed sticks, pebbles set in a pattern, sun dials or leaves anchored down with stones. Subsequent clues are at each point (write on the backs of maps or dye paper in tea to look like old charts) or print out on the computer with the clue hidden by a load of gobbledegook. Have small prizes for each team member.

BUG CATCHING

Devise a game where explorers have to catch the most interesting insect – have a book to hand to enable identification and encourage players to make up a story about the adventure they had when they were hunting for the rare insect in the jungle.

RELAY RACE

Divide into two teams. When it's your turn put on the rucksack, run to a point and pick up an object (wild animal stuffed toy, map, compass, sleeping bag etc), put it into the rucksack, run back and pass the rucksack to the next member of the team.

THE STALKING GAME

Have quiet stalking games with the 'hunter' blind-folded.

SLEEPING LIONS

This is a great game for trying to quieten over-excited guests before the meal or going home time. Everyone has to lie completely still. The first to wriggle or make a noise is out and then helps the judge to check the other contestants (tickling is good for provoking a response!).

CUNNING CLOTHES PEGS

A good game for young children is hunt the coloured clothes peg. These are pegged to leaves, washing lines, flower pots and other more hidden locations. Each child has to gather as many as possible and perhaps one of each colour, within a time limit. For older children, make a list with pictures of different leaves, flowers or birds. Attach photocopies of the different items with clothes pegs as before. Each child has to collect the full set of pictures and match up correctly to the list. (Use a child's encyclopedia or CD-ROM for ideas and lists.)

ANIMAL MASKS

An ideal activity for rainy days when explorers cannot play in the garden. You can make a whole zoo of wild animals! They are made from paper plates and bowls, empty salad or yoghurt pots (especially those ones with divided corners for fruit), egg boxes, tissue paper, straws and crêpe paper. Staple the muzzles onto the plate and stick or glue egg boxes or circles for the eyes (this can be done in advance). Children

can stick on tissue and crêpe paper to decorate the noses and faces. Scrunched up tissue looks like fur and strips of paper make great whiskers. Paint on eyes with poster paint. For ears, cut a circle from paper, make a snip from the edge to the centre and overlap to form a curved ear. Staple to the plate.

THE FISHING GAME

Cut tropical fish from brightly coloured paper. Give each fish different scores, e.g. 5, 10, 25. Stick on a small fridge magnet (available in packs from art and craft suppliers). Make a fishing rod from a stick with a string and magnet attached. Throw all the fish onto a sheet of blue paper (the 'Blue Lagoon'). Contestants each have to fish in turn against the clock. Highest score wins.

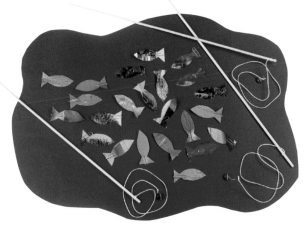

ESSENTIAL EXPLORERS' EQUIPMENT

For an outdoor adventure party, practical clothing is a must, especially if you are going for a walk. Don't forget waterproofs, a fleece for warmth, comfortable shoes and a sun hat (remember to put these requirements on the invitation). Other good ideas are binoculars, a compass, a disposable camera or two and a magnifying glass so everyone can be involved. Children should also have a rucksack in which you can put iron rations such as a bottle of drink, some fruit and biscuits. Adults accompanying the explorers should also take sun tan lotion, a map and a mobile phone.

MAKE AN EXPLORERS' CAMP

For a small group of older children (over tens), extend the fun by sleeping out under the stars or in a tent. This separates the men from the boys as the family cat or local hedgehog is bound to produce squeals and shrieks and the average suburban garden at night suddenly seems like a vast forest miles from civilization.

EXPLORERS' RATIONS

Food can be a picnic or barbecue. Having a bonfire for toasting marshmallows or similar and hot chocolate is always a winner. Serve food on leaf plates and bowls (available at Asian supermarkets).

GOODY BAGS

Make goody bags from camouflage material, old maps folded and stuck to form paper bags, or jungle print paper. The contents can include anything which encourages adventure – small compass, energy or cereal snack bars, pull-top bottles of spring water, book of adventure stories, snapstick light (available from camping stores), thick 'hiking' socks, tiny travel toothbrush/toothpaste (get a frequent traveller to collect freebies on plane journeys!) plus a notebook and twig pencil for recording tales of daring adventure.

Other sources of inspiration

• Army surplus stores for fancy dress.

• Camping and outdoor adventure stores.

• Very young children will enjoy a wild safari. Hide lots of soft animal toys in the garden for them to find.

• Older children will get the same high with an orienteering event, arranged in the local park. Remember to have plenty of adult helpers at the check-in points with mobile phones and set strict boundaries (i.e. within the park).

• For teenagers, war games or paint balling sessions are ideal. These can be arranged indoors or outside. Look up Paintball and Combat Games in the telephone directory.

'DR LIVINGSTONE, I PRESUME?'

CATERPILLAR

A cake children will love and there's
no cooking involved!

INGREDIENTS
10 mini Swiss rolls (approx)
$1/2$ quantity buttercream for 'gluing'
(see page 20)
4 tubes chocolate sweets
1 round chocolate biscuit
White and milk chocolate buttons
Jellybeans
2 candy sticks (sweet cigarettes)
50g (2oz) green-coloured coconut
(see page 23)

EQUIPMENT
30cm (12in) round cake board
Sharp knife
Teaspoon

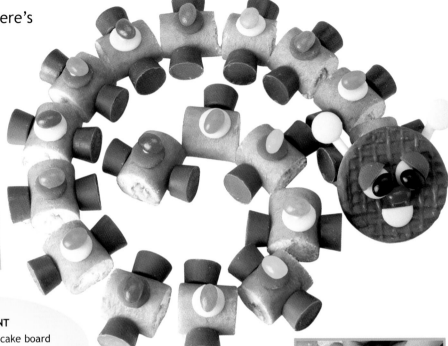

2 Stick two chocolate
sweets either side of
each roll for legs.
Again, use buttercream to
hold them in place. Stick
a chocolate button and
jellybean on the top of
each roll.

1 Slice the Swiss rolls in half and position them
around the board in a coiled arrangement. Stick
each in place with a dab of buttercream.

4 Stick the head in position leaning against the first Swiss roll. To make the feelers, stick two white chocolate buttons on the ends of two candy sticks. Either poke the feelers into or rest against the Swiss roll behind the head.

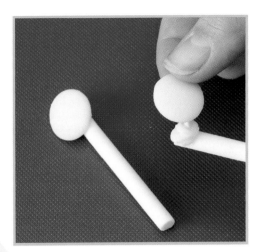

3 To make the head, stick two white chocolate buttons on top of a chocolate biscuit for eyes. Cut another white button in half for his mouth. Cut a milk chocolate button in half for eyelids. Add jellybeans for pupils and nose.

TIP
If you spread any leftover buttercream around the edges of the cake board before sprinkling the coconut, the icing will glue the coconut down and stop it falling everywhere!

5 To finish, spoon the coloured coconut around the board.

DINOSAUR ISLAND

Very dramatic but easy to put together. This is the sort of Dinosaur Island not to be frightened of!

INGREDIENTS
20cm (8in) round sponge cake (see page 17)
2 quantities buttercream (see page 20)
Black, green and blue food colour pastes
Brown food paste or teaspoon of cocoa
45g (1^1/$_2$ oz) green-coloured ready-to-roll icing or marzipan
2 tbsp soft, light brown sugar

EQUIPMENT
25cm (10in) round cake board
Carving knife
Palette knife
Small bowls
Fork
Garlic press (washed!)
Small sharp knife
Teaspoon
Plastic dinosaurs

2 Slice the cake in half horizontally and fill the centre with buttercream. You can use plain or coloured buttercream. Place the top layer of cake back in place. Put about 2 tablespoons of vanilla buttercream into a small bowl and partially mix in a little black food colour. Carefully spread this over the cliff area at the front of the cake.

3 Colour about 5 tablespoons of buttercream green and spread this over the rest of the cake. When the cake is covered, you can use a fork to rough it up slightly to look like vegetation. If you want to add a bit of 'mud', colour a tablespoon of buttercream brown using food colour or a little cocoa powder.

1 Start by carving the cake into an irregular island shape. Cut a curve out of the front of the cake for the beach area and a few lumps out of the sides and top. You can use some of the cutaway pieces to form small hills on top and around the cake.

4 Place about 3 tablespoons of buttercream in another bowl and partially mix in a little blue food colour. Spread this around the cake board, leaving a space for the sand.

5 Place a little of the green-coloured ready-to-roll icing or marzipan into the garlic press and squeeze. Slice off the strands with a knife and stick them around the cake. Vary the lengths of these strands.

6 To finish, carefully spoon the sugar into the space beneath the cliffs to make a beach and place the dinosaurs around the island.

TIP
If you leave out the dinosaurs, you can easily turn this design into a desert island cake.

DRAGON

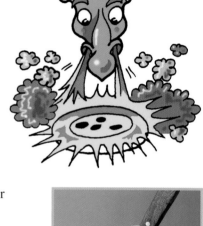

There shouldn't be too much of a battle between the knights around your table to dispose of this fearsome dragon at teatime!

INGREDIENTS
1 mixing bowl cake (see page 18)
2 quantities green-coloured buttercream (see page 20)
500g (1lb 2oz) green-coloured marzipan or
ready-to-roll icing (see page 21)
6–8 thin chocolate squares or biscuits
1 sheet rice paper
Black edible food pen
150g (5oz) grey-coloured coconut
(see page 23)

EQUIPMENT
Carving knife
30cm (12in) square cake board
Palette knife
Piping nozzle or small lid
Small knife
Paintbrush
Scissors

1 Slice the cake horizontally two or three times and reassemble it sandwiching the layers together with the green buttercream. Place the cake onto the board and spread a thick coating of buttercream over the outside of the cake.

2 Using the end of the palette knife press scales into the buttercream. Start around the base of the cake and work your way up.

3 Make a 120g (4oz) marzipan ball for the dragon's rear leg and a 90g (3oz) ball for his front. Squash the balls slightly and stick up against the dragon's body. Make scales on the legs by pressing a piping nozzle or small lid held at an angle into the marzipan.

4 Use about 150g (5oz) marzipan for his tail. Save a little for the triangular pointy bit on the end and roll the rest into a tail about 30cm (12in) long. Lay the tail in place with the thinnest part at the front of the cake. Make scales as before. Make and stick a triangle on the end of the tail.

5 Use the rest of the marzipan for his head. Put a little bit to one side for his ears and roll the rest into a tapering sausage shape. Make a cut for his mouth, place the head in position and make scales as before.

6 Make two little triangles for ears and, using the end of a paintbrush, poke a hollow in each ear and two nostrils in his nose. Stick the ears in place with a little water. Carefully slice the chocolate squares or biscuits in half into triangles and stick upright along his body and tail.

7 Draw the eyes, smoke and wings onto rice paper using the food pen and carefully cut them out. Place the eyes on the head and hold them in place with tiny curved bits of marzipan eyebrows. (Don't use water or they'll melt!) Poke the smoke into a nostril. Place the wings in place on his back and cut out some tiny triangles for teeth. If the teeth won't stand up, make tiny slits with a knife in his jaw and insert a tooth in each one.

8 Smear any leftover buttercream around the base of the cake and spoon the coloured coconut around the board.

ROCKET MAN

There's no cooking at all with this design! However if you can't find (or don't like) Swiss roll, bake a cake in a rectangular loaf tin and carve a little off the corners to give it a rounded shape. After cutting out the space hatch, cover the outside with buttercream.

INGREDIENTS
Swiss roll
Ice cream cone
$1/2$ quantity buttercream (see page 20)
Small round sweets
3 marshmallows
3 milk chocolate buttons
75g ($2^1/2$oz) white marzipan
Pink or red food colour paste
Icing sugar (to stop fingers getting sticky)
Black food colour pen or black food paste
4 chocolate squares or biscuits
Flying saucer sweets
(optional – see the Tip box opposite)

EQUIPMENT
25cm (10in) square cake board
Circle cutter (optional)
Small sharp knife
Fine paintbrush (if using food colour for eyes)
Piping nozzle or small lid for making mouth

2 Stick the ice cream cone onto the front of the rocket with buttercream. Support it from below with a small ball of marzipan if necessary. Stick a line of sweets around the cone to hide the join.

1 Place the Swiss roll diagonally on the cake board. Using a circle cutter or a sharp knife, cut a disc out of the top of the roll.

66

3 Stick three marshmallows on the end of the rocket in a triangular formation and stick a chocolate button onto each marshmallow. Stick a line of sweets around the rear of the rocket.

4 To make the spaceman, roll about 45g (1^1/$_2$oz) white marzipan into a ball for the head. Also make two 10g (^{1}/$_2$oz) sausage shapes for his arms. Press a couple of lines into each arm with the back of a knife.

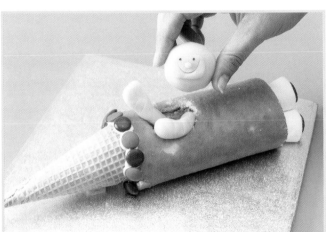

5 Colour a tiny bit of marzipan pink and squash it. Cut out a rectangle and stick onto the front of his helmet. Use the edge of a piping nozzle or cutter to press a smile into the face. Add a tiny ball for his nose and two black food colour dots for eyes.

6 Place the arms into the top of the cake. Place the head on top so he looks as though he's waving.

7 Cut chocolate squares or biscuits into rectangles and stick these around the rear of the rocket. Decorate the rest of the cake with additional sweets and sprinkle the board with flying saucer sweets.

TIP
If you can't get hold of flying saucer sweets, any sweets will do. Nobody will complain!

PRINCESSES AND SLEEPOVERS

All children believe they are beautiful princesses or daring knights. Encourage this imaginative play with a princess party which can continue long into the night with a sleepover.

SETTING THE SCENE

You want to create the illusion of a fairytale world. This can be done inside or out and the magic ingredient is a large amount of nylon netting. This costs pennies, so be generous with quantities. Hang from the ceiling to create a tented look. Create a princess throne by painting or spraying a junk shop chair in gold and swathe with a cheap feather boa. Wrap cushions in squares of satin lining fabric and tie opposite ends to secure.

Cover the tea table with a paper cloth and decorate with a satin runner, cheap sari or confetti and a layer of net on top.

Mood music is vital to set the scene.

As guests arrive, let them each chose from the dressing up box of frippery – ballerina tutus, chiffon scarves and lengths of satin lining. Wands and tiaras are essential – ensure there is one for each guest (these can be taken home after the party).

ACTIVITIES

PRINCESS AND THE PEA

The peas are ping pong balls. Two players take part and the object of the game is to collect as many peas as possible. Throw the peas (use about fifteen) about the room. At one end there are two chairs with small bowls. Each player has a spoon and picks up the balls without using their other hand and fills their bowl. An alternative is to suck through straws to pick up the ping pong balls. The winner is the child with the greatest number of peas.

STORY PRINCESS

Any adult who is a good story teller can take on this role. Dress up as a medieval princess and sit on a decorated throne. All the children gather round and are told a story. You can alternate between stories that invite audience participation and updated classics that could quieten things down at the end of the party.

SLUMBER PARTIES

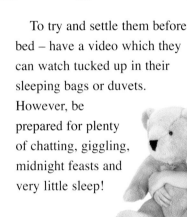

An ideal activity for girls is a beauty salon makeover, in which they can style their hair and apply simple make-up such as nail polish, lip gloss and body glitter. Remember to have plenty of cotton wool and make-up remover to hand!

Another idea is a DIY Fashion Week. Provide white bin bags, masses of crêpe paper, sticky tape, scissors, feathers and other trimmings. Have a time limit and challenge each guest to come up with an original outfit.

Some sort of craft activity is always a good idea, such as bead jewellery making or decorating boxes with jewels and trimmings as treasure boxes. Why not have a fashion parade and record each model on film?

To try and settle them before bed – have a video which they can watch tucked up in their sleeping bags or duvets. However, be prepared for plenty of chatting, giggling, midnight feasts and very little sleep!

GOODY BAGS

For a princess party, make up dolly bags from several layers of net or tissue paper and clear cellophane. Contents should be sparkly wherever possible. Ideas for gifts include small jewellery bead kits; glitter glue and small notebooks; inexpensive plastic jewellery; sparkle hair or body glitter; pretty pastel coloured sweets; lamé scrunchies and tiaras; bath cubes; lip gloss and hair gel.

OTHER IDEAS

How about a castle party? This is particularly good for a mixed group of boys and girls. Get four large cardboard boxes from your local electrical or furniture store. Cut to form a castellated profile for the four towers. Stretch corrugated card or brown paper between the towers. Activities can include dressing up as knights in crêpe paper tabards or damsels in conical hats, painting shields, and charging around as jousting knights. Have an archery tournament with sucker-type arrows. As an alternative to a castle, create a tented pavilion (adapt summer canvas gazebos), decorated with pennants and plenty of cushions.

REAL FAIRY CAKES

Equipment
Fine paintbrush
Scissors
3 piping bags or small
polythene food bags

These fairies will bring a bit of magic to the party! You could even make the cake decorating part of the celebration so that everyone makes their own fairy.

Ingredients
Glacé icing (see page 21)
or ready-to-roll icing for topping cakes (see left)
Icing sugar for rolling out
Water for sticking ready-to-roll icing
150g (5oz) flesh-coloured ready-to-roll
icing (use paprika, or a mixture of pink and
yellow food pastes to make a light skin tone;
use brown food colour for darker shades)
150g (5oz) white ready-to-roll icing
150g (5oz) pink ready-to-roll icing
150g (5oz) yellow ready-to-roll icing
2 sheets rice paper
Black food colour pen or black (liquorice)
food colour paste
4 tbsp buttercream or royal icing, or writing
icing (see TIP opposite) for the hair
Edible silver or gold balls

Top your fairy cakes first with a spoonful of glacé icing or a ready-to-roll icing disc. You will need about 150g (5oz) coloured ready-to-roll icing for topping 24 cakes. Use a circle cutter or a lid to cut out the discs. If the discs will not stick to the top of the cake, 'glue' them in place with a dab of buttercream, jam or water.

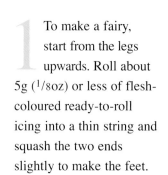

1 To make a fairy, start from the legs upwards. Roll about 5g (¹/8oz) or less of flesh-coloured ready-to-roll icing into a thin string and squash the two ends slightly to make the feet.

2 Bend the legs into a horseshoe shape and stick on the top of a cake. If you have used glacé icing, the legs will sink into the icing. If you have used ready-to-roll icing, stick the legs in place with a dab of water. Tweak the feet up slightly.

3 Roll 5g (¹/8oz) of pink, white or yellow ready-to-roll icing into a pointed conical shape for the fairy's body and flatten the top slightly ready for the head. Use a dab of water to stick the body onto the legs.

4 Make a tiny flesh-coloured ball for the fairy's head and two teeny-weeny sausage shapes for her arms. Stick the head on top of the body and the arms against the sides of her body or in whatever position you wish.

5 Fold a piece of rice paper in half and cut out a wing shape along the fold. When you open it out, it should form a heart shape. Gently press the fold of the wings into the back of the fairy to leave a small groove down her back. Paint a *light* line of water down the groove and carefully press the wings into position and open slightly. Don't soak the fairy's back or her wings will dissolve!

TIP
Look for packets of 'Writing Icing' at the supermarket. These contain tubes of ready-coloured icing. The yellow and black tubes are ideal for piping hair with minimal fuss.

6 Place a little coloured buttercream or royal icing into a piping bag or small polythene food bag. Snip a tiny triangle off the end and pipe hair over the fairy's head. Finish her off by pressing two or three edible silver balls onto the top of her head.

7 Give the fairy two dots for eyes using either a black food colour pen or black food colour and a fine paintbrush.

Variations
Add couple of tablespoons of hundreds and thousands to the raw cake mixture to give your cakes a rainbow effect when cooked. Or try adding some chocolate chips or a little pink food colour. Make mini cakes by using a mini muffin tray and petit fours paper cases.

DREAM CASTLE

Don't quake with fear if your child asks for a castle cake this year as not only is this design stunning to look at, but it's easy to build as well.

INGREDIENTS
15cm (6in) round sponge cake (see page 17)
1 quantity buttercream (see page 20)
4 chocolate Swiss rolls
Edible silver ball
4 ice cream cones
Mini-marshmallows
4 finger biscuits
1 sheet rice paper
Assorted sweets and lollipops for centre and board

EQUIPMENT
30cm (12in) round cake board
Carving knife
Palette knife
Small sharp knife
Piping bags (optional)
Scissors

TIP
If you buy a ready-made sponge cake for the centre cake, you could put this castle together in an afternoon without going anywhere near an oven!

1 Split the sponge cake in half and fill with buttercream. Place the cake in the centre of the board and spread a thick layer of buttercream over the sides and top. Stand the Swiss rolls upright in position around the cake. Use extra buttercream to secure them if necessary.

2 Cut five chocolate sticks to size to make the front door and press into the front of the cake. Finish off with an edible silver ball door knocker, stuck with a dab of buttercream.

3 Stick a cone on top of each Swiss roll. Use a liberal dose of buttercream to secure each cone in place.

4 Stick mini-marshmallows around the edge of each roof, the top of the centre cake and around the base of the cake.

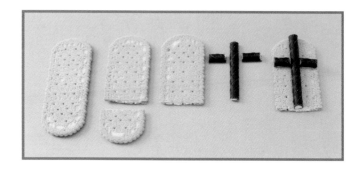

5 To make a window, cut a short section off a finger biscuit. (Score it first, then snap.) Stick one long section of chocolate stick down the centre of the biscuit with buttercream and two shorter bits either side. Stick onto a Swiss roll. Make one window for each turret.

6 Cut four small triangles out of rice paper and stick one on the top of each roof with a dab of buttercream. Decorate the sides of the tower with sweets and pile a heap of sweets and lollipops in the middle. Sprinkle small round sweets around the base to resemble cobblestones.

RAG DOLL

Well, hello Dolly! A ribbon always adds a bit of elegance to a cake. It also hides any messy bits around the sides and base!

Trace this panel and use as template for doll's dress

INGREDIENTS
20cm (8in) round sponge cake
(see page 17)
1 quantity vanilla buttercream (see page 20)
Icing sugar for rolling out on
500g (1lb 2oz) white ready-to-roll icing
(see page 21)
2 plain round biscuits
4 trifle sponge fingers
Pink food colour paste
2 white chocolate buttons
2 round red sweets
Cola-flavoured bootlace sweets
Strawberry-flavoured lace sweets
Strawberry-flavoured bootlace sweets
Additional sweets for decoration

EQUIPMENT
25cm (10in) round cake board
Carving knife
Palette knife
Rolling pin
Small sharp knife
Dress template (see panel above)
Paintbrush
1m (36in) ribbon
Scissors
Sticky tape

1 Level the top of the cake and turn it upside down. Split and fill the middle of the cake with buttercream. Place it in the middle of the cake board and spread buttercream around the sides and top.

2 Dust the worksurface with icing sugar and knead and roll out the ready-to-roll icing. Place the icing over the top of the cake and smooth into position. Trim and neaten the base. Keep the excess icing and colour it pale pink for the doll's dress.

3 Place the two biscuits in position for the head and body. Glue with buttercream.

4 Lay two trifle sponges in place for her legs. Again, secure with buttercream.

5 Roll out the pink icing. Trace the shape of the panel, left, cut it out and lay the dress template on top of the pink icing and cut around it. Press lines into the lower part of the dress with a paintbrush.

6 Cut two trifle sponges to size for her arms. Stick white chocolate buttons on her head for eyes. Add two tiny sections of cola-flavoured lace for pupils.

7 Use a dab of water to stick tiny section of strawberry bootlace for a mouth. Add two red sweets for cheeks.

8 Twist two strawberry-flavoured laces together to make the hair. Stick them against each side of the head with buttercream and tie a bow with a length of strawberry bootlace. Repeat on the other side.

9 Make and stick a bow of strawberry bootlace onto the front of her dress. Place a length of ribbon around the side of the cake and secure one end on top of the other with sticky tape. Glue sweets around the doll with buttercream.

TIP
If you can't get find bootlace sweets, use strands of ready-to-roll icing instead.

SQUASHED TEDDY BEARS

As well as for birthdays, this design could also be used as a cute Christening cake. You can use ready-to-roll icing for the teddy bears if you do not like the taste of marzipan.

INGREDIENTS

1 x 18cm (7in) round cake cut in half or two 18cm (7in) cakes baked in sandwich tins (use the 3-egg recipe on page 17)
1 quantity vanilla buttercream (see page 20)
500g (1lb 2oz) golden marzipan
30g (1oz) white marzipan (see TIP below)
Icing sugar to stop fingers getting sticky
Black food colour pen or black food colour paste
Hundreds and thousands

EQUIPMENT

25cm (10in) round cake board
Palette knife
Fine paintbrush
Piping nozzle or small lid

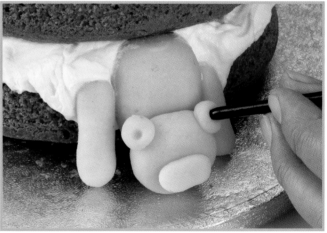

1. Place one layer on the cake board and spread a liberal coating of buttercream over the cake. Place the second layer on top.

TIP

Buy one 500g (1lb 2oz) pack of white marzipan, retain about 30g (1oz) for the muzzles and colour the rest using food colouring.

2. To make a teddy poking out head first, start with his body. Roll about 20g (^{3}/4oz) marzipan into an oval. Push it into the icing between the two cakes. Roll about 15g (^{1}/2oz) marzipan into a ball for his head and stick onto the body. Use a dab of water to help the pieces stick together if necessary.

3. Add two little sausage shapes for arms and two tiny ball shapes for ears. Make a hollow in each ear with the end of a paintbrush.

4. Add an oval of white marzipan for his muzzle and make a little hollow in that for his mouth. An alternative way to make a mouth is by pressing the edge of a piping nozzle into the marzipan to make either a smile or a frown.

5 Add two black dots for eyes and one for a nose using either a black food colour pen or black food colour and a fine paintbrush.

6 To make the teddies reversing out of the cake, roll about 20g (^{3}/4oz) marzipan into an oval shape for a body. Again push this into the icing between the layers. Add two small sausage shapes for legs, bending the end of each sausage into an 'L' shape for feet.

7 When you have put teddies all around the middle of the cake, spread the top of the cake with buttercream and make the top teddy. In case he goes wrong, make him up off the cake and stick him in place when he's finished.

8 Roll about 30g (1oz) marzipan into an oval for his body and stand it upright. Add a smaller ball for his head and sausage shapes for the legs.

9 Make a face and ears as before and make two smaller sausage shapes for arms. Stick one of these pointing upwards. Bend the hand forwards slightly to make it look as though he's waving.

10 Finally, place the teddy in position on top of the cake and sprinkle a few hundreds and thousands around him.

BOWL OF POPCORN

You don't have to fill your bowl with just popcorn – you could substitute sweets or breakfast cereals instead.

EQUIPMENT
Carving knife
Palette knife
20cm (8in) square cake board
Rolling pin
Heart-shaped cutter
(optional)
Paintbrush

INGREDIENTS
1 pudding bowl cake (see page 17)
1 quantity buttercream (see page 20)
500g (1lb 2oz) green-coloured
ready-to-roll icing or marzipan
Icing sugar for rolling out on
Sugar-coated chocolate drops or small sweets
Sweet popcorn

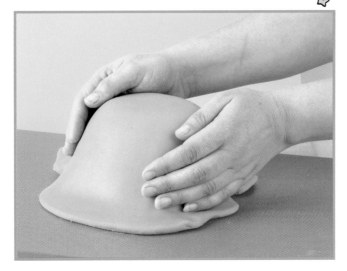

3 Place a small dollop of buttercream in the centre of the cake board to hold the cake in place. Turn the covered cake the right way up so that it now looks like a bowl and place it in position.

1 Level the top of the cake if necessary. Then turn the cake over so that it is now standing on its widest part. Slice it horizontally two or three times and reassemble, sandwiching it together with buttercream. Spread a thin coating of buttercream around the outside of the cake.

2 Knead the green icing or marzipan until pliable. Dust your worksurface with icing sugar and roll the icing out. Lift and place it over the cake and smooth the top and sides. Trim away and keep the excess.

4 Gently press a heart-shaped cutter into the icing to make a pattern. Try not to go right through or the buttercream may leak through.

5 Paint a line of water around the top edge of the bowl. Roll the leftover green icing into a long string and lay this around the edge of the bowl to make a neat rim.

6 Using little dabs of buttercream as glue, stick a line of sweets around the rim of the bowl to neaten the join.

7 Get rid of any dusty icing sugar marks by gently brushing with a soft, damp paintbrush. Fill up your bowl with popcorn.

TIP
If you don't have a heart cutter, you could use a small round lid instead to make a circular design. Alternatively you could always leave it plain.

GINGERBREAD HOUSE

Don't be put off by first impressions and think that this is too complicated to make. Some steps can be done in advance to save a mad rush on party day.

The gingerbread dough can be kept in the fridge for up to three days. The baked house sections can be kept in a plastic airtight container for about three days. Once the house is built, it should keep in a box in a dry place for at least a week (that is if no-one nibbles it!).

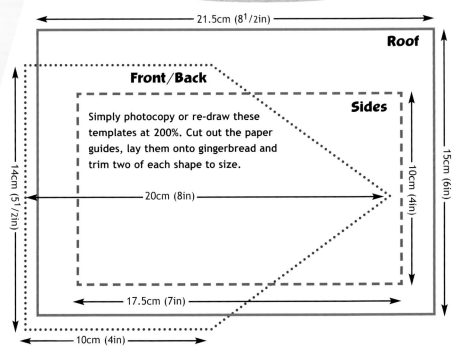

INGREDIENTS
Gingerbread dough (see page 20)
1 quantity royal icing (see page 21)
Assorted mini marshmallows and small sweets
Battenburg cake or square biscuits for windows
Milk and white chocolate finger biscuits
Edible silver ball for door knocker
Round flat sweets or biscuits for roof tiles
Long marshmallow sweet for ridge of roof (optional)
2 wafer biscuits for chimney
50g (1^1/2oz) green-coloured coconut (see page 23)

EQUIPMENT
Tin foil
Baking trays
Cling film
Rolling pin
Baking parchment or greaseproof templates for walls and roof (see guides right)
Sharp knife
30cm (12in) round cake board
2 cups or glasses
Piping bags (optional)

21.5cm (8^1/2in)

Roof

Front/Back

Sides

Simply photocopy or re-draw these templates at 200%. Cut out the paper guides, lay them onto gingerbread and trim two of each shape to size.

14cm (5^1/2in)

20cm (8in)

15cm (6in)

10cm (4in)

17.5cm (7in)

10cm (4in)

1 Pre-heat the oven to 170°C/ 325°F/ Gas mark 3. Place a piece of tin foil the same size as your baking tray on your worksurface. Place a quarter of the gingerbread dough on top and lay a sheet of cling film on top of the dough (this will stop the dough sticking to your rolling pin). Roll out the dough to a thickness of about 1cm ($^{1}/_{4}$in) and remove the cling film. Place a wall or roof template on top and cut around it using a sharp knife and remove excess. Holding the tin foil at the edges, transfer the gingerbread on the foil on to the baking tray. Bake for 15-25 minutes until the gingerbread is firm to the touch and dark around the edges. Leave to cool then gently peel away the foil. Repeat the process making two roof sections, two pointed walls and two rectangular wall sections.

2 To build your house, start with the sides. Pipe or use a knife to smear a line of royal icing along the base and sides of a front and side wall. Stand them upright on the cake board. Stick the remaining two sections in place. If you have time, leave these to dry for a few hours. Stick the roof sections in place and use two cups or glasses to take the weight and stop them slipping while they dry.

3 When dry, pipe or use a knife to smear additional royal icing along all the joins then stick mini-marshmallows or small sweets along the sides. To make the windows, use thin slices of Battenburg cake or square biscuits. Glue in place with royal icing.

4 To make the door, stick four milk chocolate fingers upright at the front and three white chocolate finger biscuits around the sides. Use another two white chocolate biscuits on top of each other for steps. Finish the door off with a gleaming edible silver ball door knocker. Fill in the brickwork around the doors and windows with small sweets.

5 Decorate the roof one side at a time. Stick a line of flat sweets or biscuits along the bottom edge of the roof. Repeat another line above allowing them to overlap the first. Continue all over the roof. Repeat on the other side. Lie a long marshmallow sweet or line of sweets along the ridge of the roof and add extra colourful sweets or marshmallows along the eaves to hide any joins.

6 Make a chimney by sticking two wafer biscuits together. Slice a section off at an angle so that it sits snugly on the roof and glue in place with more icing. Stick a small rounded sweet on top for a chimney pot. Finish by scattering green-coloured coconut grass and a few more sweets around the base of the house.

CHRISTMAS VARIATION

This version uses biscuits as tiles which is much quicker than fiddling around with all those sweets! Apart from that, it is built in exactly the same way except that the colours have been limited to red, green and white.

Once the house is assembled, some watered-down royal icing is carefully spooned over the roof to look like snow. The icing is also encouraged to drip to look like icicles. Icing 'snow' is then smeared around the cake board and a few marshmallow snowballs are piled up against the house.

GAMES AND ACTIVITIES

BEACH RELAY RACES

Divide into two teams. Each contestant has to run to a marker, then run around this three times holding onto the pole and with their head bent. When they try to run back they'll be very wobbly, having run round in circles!

FLAP THE KIPPER

Cut small kippers from light-weight paper (tissue paper is ideal). Cut eight 10cm (4in) 'flappers' from cards. Rather like tiddlywinks, the object is to flap the kipper along the ground to the finishing line by creating a draught. Divide into teams with timed heats, or have a general free-for-all.

ON THE TOWEL

The old standby of 'on the rug, off the rug' can be given a tropical twist with a brightly coloured beach towel or two. This burns up a lot of energy jumping on and off and can be repeated as it is a quick time filler for five minutes.

DANCING

Hawaiian dancing and limbo dancing are always popular activities. Boys and girls will enjoy a lively limbo dancing competition to the sound of Caribbean music.

TEAM GAMES

Volleyball, badminton and beach skittles are all good outside games.

COCONUT SHY

Set up various targets – they don't all have to be coconuts! Each target can be marked with a different number of points depending on how difficult it is to hit with the ball. Each player throws four balls and the winner is the child with the highest score who may then choose a prize. Prizes could include funny sunglasses, floral hair accessories, small packs of coloured pencils or crayons, or a small tube of sunscreen.

'IN THE SUMMERTIME WHEN THE WEATHER IS FINE'

Goody bags

Use crêpe paper sacks filled with small blow-up plastic balls, tropical fruit drinks, diving goggles, shells, exotic hair clips and funny sunglasses. Teenagers could receive a fragrant tealight and holder or a lip balm tied up in a wisp of dyed muslin or net.

OTHER SOURCES OF INSPIRATION

• This party can be a real mix of cultures, so if you live somewhere which has Indian textile stores or Oriental supermarkets, look there for ideas – inexpensive saris for use as tablecloths, paper Chinese lanterns, incense sticks.
• Check out sports stores and fashion shops, specialising in 'surf style' for ex-display material that you may be able to recycle (full-size palm trees for example!).
• Look in travel brochures for other ideas on colours and motifs.

BEACH PARTY FOOD AND DRINKS

Food can be barbecued or prepared in the kitchen and served on skewers (chicken satay sticks or fruit kebabs are always popular). Serve exotic-looking non-alcoholic cocktails or fruit smoothies in tall glasses with garnishes, umbrellas and bendy straws. Use brightly coloured paper tableware or plastic and acrylic partyware. Remember that clashing colours and patterns are the desired effect.

For a Bali-high atmosphere, eat the birthday tea seated on cushions around a low table near the ground. With older children, it is probably safe to have candles in containers or hanging lanterns.

KIDS' COCKTAILS

A fun activity is to have an adult bartender mixing up exotic concoctions for party guests. The essential features for any cocktail are a dramatic name, outrageous colour and fun accessories including neon coloured bendy straws, cocktail umbrellas and garnishes of fruit, such as pineapple, orange, banana, seedless grapes and kiwi fruit. Create dramatic dyed icecubes with food colouring. Limequats (baby limes) can be sliced into two and frozen as an alternative ice cube. Use brightly coloured acrylic or plastic tumblers and these can be included in the goody bags after washing.

SUNDOWNER
Pour pure orange juice into a tall glass. Gently pour in some cranberry juice. The red fruit juice slowly works through the orange producing a dramatic sunset effect.

LIME TIME
This can be limeade or apple juice served 'straight up'. Garnish with green accessories and green grapes, apple chunks and kiwi slices.

RED ALERT
For a traffic-stopping drink, first place in the glass a strawberry, then slice of orange, green grape and so on until the glass is almost full. Slowly pour on cherryade so that it soaks through the layers. Provide an umbrella or spoon so that the traffic light fruit can be scooped up and eaten.

BLUE LAGOON

First dip the rim of the glass in lemon juice and then press the upturned glass into coloured sugar (using sugar shaken with food colouring in a jam jar). Colour lemonade with blue food colouring. Wrap the top end of a long kebab skewer with a strip of green crêpe paper, stick with a tiny piece of clear tape and fringe to look like a palm tree. Thread the skewer with pineapple, orange and pineapple chunks and pop into the drink just before serving.

Remember that fizzy children's drinks are usually available sugar-free and additive-free, but as an alternative you can always colour lemonade with food colourings.

ICE-CREAM PARLOUR

Another birthday tea treat that is always popular is to set up a pretend ice-cream parlour. You'll need at least half a dozen soft scoop ice-cream varieties of different colours such as chocolate, mint choc chip, toffee, strawberry, raspberry ripple and lemon sorbet. Don't forget the old favourite vanilla for good measure. Buy an assortment of wafer fans, chocolate wafer curls and coloured sprinkles, fruit toppings and chopped nuts (be careful of food allergies) and have bowls of fruit such as sliced bananas, raspberries and peaches. Let the children choose their combination of fruit, ice-cream and toppings and serve in classic pressed glass sundae dishes or brightly coloured picnicware with long-handled spoons.

PINEAPPLE

You'll find it easier to decorate this cake using a nylon piping bag and a large star piping nozzle. The nylon bag is stronger than greaseproof paper so won't burst or tear. If you can't get hold of one, you could cover the pineapple with thick orange buttercream and use the flat of a palette knife to tweak the icing into peaks.

INGREDIENTS
Mixing bowl cake
(see page 18)
2 quantities buttercream
(see page 20)
(Colour 3/4 orange using either orange or a mixture of yellow and red food colour. Colour the remaining buttercream green.)
100g (4oz) light brown muscovado sugar

EQUIPMENT
Carving knife
Palette knife
30cm (12in) square cake board
1 or 2 x 30cm (12in) nylon piping bags
(available from kitchen or cake equipment shops)
Large star piping nozzle
Cup
Kitchen paper

TIP
Once you have mastered this style of piping you can use it to decorate other shaped cakes too. For example, cover a Christmas cake with white royal icing stars to make it look as though it is covered with snowflakes.

1 Carve a little off two sides of the cake to make a pineapple shape. Split and fill the centre of the cake with orange buttercream.

2 Reassemble the cake and place it diagonally onto the cake board. Spread a layer of orange buttercream over the outside of the cake.

3 Place the large star nozzle into the piping bag and place about three tablespoons of orange buttercream into the bag. Twist the end of the bag to close it and to force the icing out of the nozzle.

TIP
Stand the piping bag in a cup or glass while you fill it. The cup will hold the bag steady, leaving both your hands free.

4 Pipe a line of stars around the base of the cake. It's easy to do. Simply squeeze, release the pressure and pull the bag away. Practice on your worktop first if you're a bit unsure.

5 Continue piping around and over the cake. Refill the piping bag when necessary.

6 Squeeze any leftover icing out of the bag and clean and dry the bag and nozzle. (Kitchen paper is good for drying bags.)

7 Put the star nozzle back into the bag and place the green buttercream into the bag. Twist and squeeze to close the bag as before.

8 To pipe strands for the leaves, squeeze the bag and continue to squeeze lightly as you pull the bag away. Release the pressure and the icing will fall away, leaving a leaf shape behind.

9 For a tropical beach look, sprinkle light brown muscovado sugar around the cake board.

WATERBABIES

This is quite a small but cute paddling pool. Feel free to make it larger if you wish by using a bigger cake.

INGREDIENTS
15cm (6in) round sponge cake (see page 17)
1 quantity vanilla buttercream (see page 20)
Blue, black, brown, yellow, green and pink or flesh (paprika) food colour pastes
White and milk chocolate finger biscuits
*100g (4oz) flesh-coloured ready-to-roll icing (see page 21)
(use paprika or a mixture of yellow and hint of pink food paste to get desired shade)
*75g (3oz) brown-coloured ready-to-roll icing
Small sweets

Increase or decrease the amounts shown here depending upon how many swimmers you want to cram into your pool!

EQUIPMENT
20cm (8in) round cake board
Carving knife
Palette knife
Small bowls
Piping nozzle or small cutter
Paintbrush
Piping bags (optional)

1 Split the cake in half horizontally and fill the centre of the cake with vanilla buttercream. Put the cake back together again.

2 Put approximately 4 tablespoons of buttercream into a bowl and partially mix in a little blue food colour. Spread this around the sides and top of the cake. Make it quite thick on the top as you want your water to look choppy!

3 Press white and milk chocolate fingers alternately around the side of the cake.

4 To make the swimmers, use about 45g (1¹/₂oz) ready-to-roll icing for each head. Roll into a ball shape and use the edge of a piping nozzle or small cutter to press a 'U' shape for a smile.

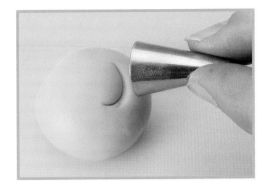

5 Stick tiny ball shapes for ears and noses in place with a little water. Make a hollow in each ear with the end of a paintbrush. Add two black food colour dots for eyes. Pipe wiggly curls or smear dabs of coloured buttercream on the top of each head for hair.

6 Make small sausage shapes for arms. Place the heads and arms into the pool. Make two sausage shapes for the legs. Flatten the ends to make feet and bend into 'L' shapes. Place into the 'water'.

7 To finish, stick sweets around the side of the pool. Colour the leftover buttercream green and smear around the cake board to look like grass.

TIP
If you're feeling really ambitious, you could make the figures resemble the children coming to the party!

ARTY PARTY

Children of all ages enjoy being creative and are eager to have a go at new arts and crafts. If you have creative friends, pull them in to help or to give some impromptu tuition.

PREPARATION

Start hoarding raw materials well in advance. Essential equipment in your creative crafts box (useful throughout the year, not just at party times) can include a variety of white and coloured papers for drawing, painting or sticking; child-safe scissors; foam sheets; wacky pipe cleaners; glue sticks; felt squares; paints; brushes; crayons; PVA glue; sticky tape and face paints.

Have plenty of newspaper for covering tables. Remember that prevention is easier than stain removal! For fabric painting, you can buy plain white cotton napkins and some white T-shirts.

INVITATIONS

Photocopy the outline of an artist's palette for the invitations for the birthday child to add the paint colours. Or buy a pack of art postcards and write the invitation on the reverse, or attach a print out with the party details.

Remember to state clearly on the invitation that activities may be messy, so children should wear play clothes and bring an apron or old shirt as a cover up. Have some extra shirts on stand-by, just in case.

Peter
is inviting all his
artistic chums to his studio for
an Arty Party to celebrate his 8th
Birthday. Wear old clothes (berets and
smocks optional!) and create your own
masterpiece to take away on
the day. The fun takes place
at 2.30 on 13th March.

RSVP
Peter Picasso Jones
Address
Telephone number

SETTING THE SCENE

With such a wealth of artistic talent at your disposal, let the party crowd decorate their own party table. A plain white paper tablecloth can be transformed with crayons, potato printing and hand prints. If you do this as soon as they arrive, it will have a chance to dry before the birthday tea. Give each child a plain white fabric napkin to be decorated with fabric crayons – the colours are fixed by ironing which should be supervised by an adult. Paper cups can be decorated with stickers and paper shapes.

Top tip!
Children spend a lot of their time 'being organized' by others at home and school. They will be quite happy, once any techniques or do's and don'ts have been explained, to get on with craft activities on their own.

GAMES AND ACTIVITIES

For a party lasting a maximum of two hours you will only need a couple of different activities. Have a mix of imaginative work (painting or drawing), messier creative work (salvage crafts, T-shirt printing, collage, modelling, stamping or hand printing) plus a one or two active party games to keep the inspiration flowing.

Ask a creative adult or teenage friend along to help out. Remember it's a party not an art lesson and the emphasis is on fun. All children will enjoy drawing using charcoal, drawing with their left hand (if right handed), drawing without taking their pencil from the sheet, blowing up balloons and drawing funny faces on them with felt tip pens or drawing using pencils or brushes attached to long sticks – all these games are easy to organize and are a hoot to try.

EDIBLE ART

Make marzipan fruits. Divide the marzipan between the children. Make a small hollow in the marzipan, add a couple (only a couple!) of drops of food colouring and continue to knead until the colour mixes in. Knead the marzipan to soften and roll into small balls. Decorate with cloves, angelica as mini stems or dust lightly in icing sugar for peaches. Paint stripes on bananas with brown food colouring and create a textured surface on oranges by rolling the fruit on a cheese grater. Admire and eat at the birthday tea!

DRAW A COW

The players must draw a cow whilst blindfolded. Starting with the eyes the players must draw a feature, drop their hand, pause, then draw another feature and so on. The winner can be the child whose cow is most recognizable but have a fun prize for the funniest drawing.

GOODY BAGS

These are easy to fill with the creations made during the afternoon. You can also include a fabric crayon, a paintbrush, small pack of pencils, hopscotch chalks, glitter glue or stickers.

MODERN ART

A modern art classic guaranteed to disappear
in a most traditional way!

INGREDIENTS
15cm x 20cm (6in x 8in) sponge cake
(see page 17)
1 quantity buttercream
(see page 20)
600g (1lb 5oz) white ready-to-roll icing
Icing sugar
Red, green, blue and yellow food colour
4 long flat chocolate bars
Smarties

EQUIPMENT
Carving knife
Palette knife
25cm (10in) square cake board
Rolling pin
Cake smoothers (optional)
Small sharp knife
Small bowls or saucers
Small paintbrushes

TIP
You don't need to buy
a special cake tin to
make a rectangular cake,
simply cut 5cm (2in)
off a 20cm (8in)
square cake.

1 Level the top of the cake
so it is flat. Don't make
the cake too deep or the
finished cake won't look authentic.
Slice it in half if you wish and fill the
centre with buttercream. Reassemble and
place it onto the cake board. Spread
buttercream around the sides and top.

2 Dust your worksurface with icing
sugar and knead the ready-to-roll
icing until it's soft and pliable. Roll
it out, then lift and place over the top of
the cake. Smooth it into place and trim
away the excess from around the base.

3 Put some watered-down food colour into a bowl. Dab a soft paintbrush into the colour and flick or splatter it onto the cake top. Repeat with the other colours.

4 Place the long flat chocolate bars on the top edges of the cake and glue in place with buttercream.

TIP
If you can't get hold of long flat chocolate bars, use flat rectangular or square biscuits to build up a frame instead.

5 Cover the edges of the board with any remaining buttercream and scatter over the Smarties.

Seasonal Parties

Celebrate the changing seasons with exciting party themes and fantastic cake designs

PARTIES FOR ALL SEASONS

Celebrating the changing seasons is a great excuse for a party! Birthdays are always eagerly awaited but even if you don't have a special occasion to celebrate, seasonal parties such as Halloween are a wonderful way to rediscover and enjoy traditional crafts and games. Children will love to spend time before the party helping you to prepare the games and food.

On the following pages are ideas for parties to fit the main school holidays. However, think up your own themes to suit the age and likes of your child. For example, as a change from a standard princess party, why not organise a May Day party? You can make an impromptu maypole by decorating a rotary washing line – simply wrap the vertical pole in strips of red and white crêpe paper and have plenty of coloured streamers hanging down. Or for an authentic maypole, paint a length of cardboard carpet tube white and attach ribbons or strips of gingham firmly to the top. Get the children to make up dances that interweave the ribbons, thus wrapping the pole.

Celebrate the coming summer with a nature walk followed by a picnic in the garden. Set the scene with a brightly coloured picnic rug, piled with comfortable cushions and a simple afternoon tea of jam sandwiches, traditional cakes, fruit salad and lemonade.

Or why not have a midwinter party to celebrate the winter solstice and the shortest day? Choose a non-Christmas theme and colour scheme as children can get overloaded with red and green at this time of year. What about a black and white penguin party? Ask all the guests to come in black and white clothes and decorate the party room to look suitably Antarctic with white and turquoise crêpe paper, clear cellophane and white card, cut out to look like icebergs.

Have craft activities such as making a wacky bow tie for their 'penguin outfit', making penguin masks, painting jam jars with glass paints to make decorative tea light holders, or decorating small fairy cakes with chocolate, white glacé icing and coloured jelly shapes (this is always hugely popular with boys and girls of a variety of ages). Incorporate any games to do with fish and finish up with a suitable story about marine life or famous explorers, depending on their age. Don't forget evocative music is so important – have nature CDs (of the wind or dolphins) playing, in order to create the right mood.

EASTER PARTY

An Easter party is an ideal theme for younger children. If you can choose a sunny day, you will be able to organize both indoor and outdoor activities.

For an Easter party theme, the most important ingredients are eggs of course, both chocolate ones and hens' eggs, but don't forget there are many other types of egg, including goose or quail eggs if you can get them. Papier mâché eggs from craft supply shops are also great for decorating. The only other items you will need to stock pile are crafts materials — see the list opposite for ideas. Remember you can never have too many glue sticks!

INVITATIONS

Have fun making combined Easter cards/invitations. There are plenty of sources of inspiration – rabbits, chicks, eggs and egg-cups. Cut shapes from felt or coloured paper and decorate with stickers, paint or scraps of ribbon.

EASTER EGG DECORATING

Another simple craft that is sure to provide hours of happy entertainment. The children can take their decorated eggs away with them and if you are having an Easter tea, they can also eat boiled eggs that you have coloured earlier.

Remember to only use food dyes on eggs that will be eaten, although decorative eggs can also be coloured using fabric powder dyes. For eggs to be eaten or when working with younger children, hard boil the eggs first. Dilute the food dyes in hot water and add a little salt or white vinegar for permanent colour. Carefully lower the egg into the dye solution and remove when the correct colour is achieved. Drain on kitchen paper and allow to dry on pin stilts (four pins stuck in a polystyrene or cork tile on which the drying egg can be balanced).

Alternatively, carefully decorate the raw egg. First blow the egg, by pricking a small hole at either end with a needle and blowing the contents into a bowl. This requires patience and is only recommended for older children. This method only needs to be used if you are planning to keep the fragile decorated eggs. Decorative eggs can also be covered in découpage papers, stamps, stickers, foils, sequins and ribbons.

MAKING EASTER BONNETS

It is traditional in many countries to wear something new and brightly coloured on Easter Sunday to herald the arrival of spring and the better weather.

Making a jazzy Easter bonnet continues this tradition and is also an excellent activity to concentrate young minds for at least 30–45 minutes. Young imaginations don't need much prompting, although it is sure to spark off ideas if adults wear hats prepared earlier. Suggest several shapes that can be made such as a cone shaped bonnet that ties under the chin, a top hat, a mob cap, pill box or a Victorian bonnet. Remember that for Easter bonnets, the rule 'More is Better' definitely applies, so encourage embellishment! Have an Easter parade when everyone is finished and take photographs. Polaroid or digital pictures can be taken away on the day. Alternatively, take a whole roll of film and post a photo to each child later.

Useful materials and decorations

- Coloured card in assorted pastel colours for the hat shapes (enough for one sheet per child)
- Crêpe paper in assorted colours
- Tissue paper (buy this in reams in popular colours such as yellow and pink or buy a multi pack for variety)
- Twirling paper ribbon and scraps of fabric ribbon
- Lengths of longer and wider ribbon (at least 80cm/32in) for the ribbon ties
- Child-safe scissors (one set per child) plus some decorative edge scissors
- Decorative pens or pastel sticks
- Paper doilies
- Glue sticks
- Sequins
- Scraps or squares of felt in assorted colours
- Other useful items – sticky tape (have several reels handy), hole punch, stapler, coloured pens, stamps and stamp pad

A basic bonnet shape

To make the bonnet shown above, see the template on page 128. Re-draw or photocopy the template to size. Fold a piece of card and place the edge marked 'fold' along the folded edge. Cut out the shape. Bring the two edges marked 'overlap' together and staple to form the bonnet shape. Decorate as desired!

ACTIVITIES

EASTER EGG HUNT

This is essential, so hide small chocolate eggs around the garden (or in the house if the weather is not good). The hiding places should not all be obvious, even if this means that you are still coming across the eggs for several days afterwards. Unwrapped eggs can be covered in little twists of tissue paper or foil tied with scraps of ribbon or raffia.

Alternatively, hide coloured boiled eggs wrapped in aluminium foil (see Easter Egg Decorating on page 102).

PAPER CUTTING

Echo the traditional paper cutting traditions of Poland by folding tissue paper in half and cutting out simple, symmetrical images of chickens, hares, lambs or flowers. Stick onto plain white card or heavy paper to create Easter cards.

EGG AND SPOON RACE

Ideal if the weather allows the children to play in the garden. To make this more difficult, combine with a three-legged race.

COUNT THE SWEETS

Fill a glass jam jar with jelly beans or Smarties and have a 'Guess the number in the jar' competition. The winner, with the closest guess, wins the jar of goodies.

MINIATURE GARDEN

Celebrate the spring by making your own tiny garden. Fill a seed tray with soil and 'plant' small bits of vegetation and flower stems in a pleasing design. A handbag mirror makes a good pond and gravel is useful for paths.

Keep damp with a water spray and the garden will last for several days.

FOX AND HEN GAME

Choose one player to be a fox. The others form a line, holding each other at the waist. The first in line is the mother hen and the rest are her chicks. The fox tries to catch the last chick in the line. The mother hen protects her chick by barring the fox with his/her outstretched arms. All the chicks help by moving the end of the line away from the fox. When the fox catches a chick, the fox child is rewarded with a chocolate egg and the players choose a new fox and mother hen. If the fox cannot catch a chick within an agreed time, a change around occurs without a prize.

SETTING THE SCENE

MAD HATTERS

Create a Mad Hatter's Tea party table with brightly coloured and contrasting table settings. Use crêpe paper for table runners, twirly ribbon and chicken cake decorations at each place setting. Finish off with narcissi, muscari or other spring flowers. Cut stems short and use glass tumblers as low vases, so that they will not get knocked over.

EGG HEAD HATS

Sew jolly egg cosies using felt. Cut two shapes, slightly larger than half the circumference of the egg and sew together with contrasting embroidery cottons. Add tassels, beads or buttons depending on what scraps are in your sewing box.

PAPER CHAINS

Make seasonal paper chains from coloured paper, tissue or newspaper. Fold long lengths of paper into zigzag sections and draw a motif on the top section. Make sure that the image touches each side of the paper, so that when it is cut out and unfolded, the chain is continuous.

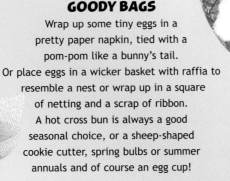

GOODY BAGS

Wrap up some tiny eggs in a pretty paper napkin, tied with a pom-pom like a bunny's tail. Or place eggs in a wicker basket with raffia to resemble a nest or wrap up in a square of netting and a scrap of ribbon. A hot cross bun is always a good seasonal choice, or a sheep-shaped cookie cutter, spring bulbs or summer annuals and of course an egg cup!

BAG OF SWEETS

Quick to make, even quicker to demolish.
What could be sweeter?

INGREDIENTS
1 pudding bowl cake (see page 17)
1 quantity buttercream
(see page 20)
Icing sugar for rolling out
500g (1lb 2oz) white
ready-to-roll icing
(see page 21)
Pink food colour paste
Sweets

EQUIPMENT
20cm (8in) square cake board
Carving knife
Palette knife
Rolling pin
Small sharp knife
Paintbrush

1 Stand the cake on the cake board so that the widest part of the cake forms the base. Split the cake horizontally two or three times and reassemble, filling the layers with buttercream. Spread a coating of buttercream over the top and sides.

2 Dust your worksurface with icing sugar and knead the icing until soft and pliable. Roll it out and cut out a rectangle approximately 43cm x 13cm (17in x 5in).

3 Slide a palette knife along under the icing to make sure it's not stuck to your worksurface. Carefully roll it up a bit like a bandage.

4 Holding the icing upright, carefully unroll it around the sides of the cake. Neaten the join and allow the top to open and gape ready for the sweets later.

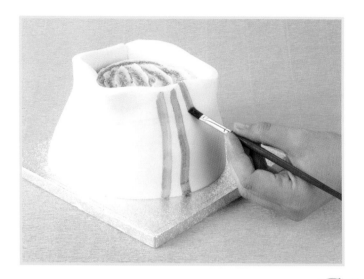

5 To decorate the cake, paint lines down the bag using a little watered-down pink food colouring.

6 To finish, fill the top of the bag with the recipient's favourite sweets.

TIP

If you don't fancy painting, you can leave the bag plain or make a pattern by pressing a decorative cutter into the icing instead (see Bowl of Popcorn on page 78).

MUCKY PUP

As well as being exceptionally easy, this design is also very versatile. To turn this cake into a rabbit, position the ear biscuits pointing upwards, use a marshmallow for a tail and two white jellybeans or mini marshmallows as teeth.

INGREDIENTS
Pudding bowl cake (see page 17)
1 quantity chocolate buttercream (see page 20)
1 round chocolate biscuit
2 round coconut biscuits or similar
2 white chocolate buttons
3 milk chocolate buttons
1 red jellybean
4 coconut (or similar) chocolate bars
3 finger biscuits
50g (1¹/₂oz) milk chocolate

EQUIPMENT
25cm (10in) round cake board
Carving knife
Palette knife
Fork
Piping bag (optional)
Heatproof bowl

1 The widest part of the cake forms the base. Slice the cake horizontally two or three times. Reassemble, filling the layers with buttercream. Position the cake towards the rear of the cake board and spread a thick layer of buttercream around the outside of the cake.

2 Use the back of a fork to rough up the icing to give the cake a furry effect.

3 Press a round chocolate biscuit onto the front of the cake to make the puppy's face. Add two round coconut biscuits for his cheeks. Using a piping bag or knife, apply additional blobs of buttercream as glue if necessary.

4 Use white and milk chocolate buttons to make the puppy's eyes and nose.

5 Add a red jellybean for his tongue and place four small chocolate bars in position for his paws. They should all be facing forwards.

6 Press two oval biscuits against the side of the head for his ears and one at his rear for his tail.

7 To make the mud for your pup to be mucky in, place the chocolate in a heatproof bowl. Melt the chocolate in a microwave oven for a minute or two, or place the bowl over a pan of simmering water. Be careful not to get any water in the chocolate though, or your mud will turn terribly gritty. Let the chocolate cool slightly, then smear around the cake board and dog to create the desired effect.

TIP
Stick additional sweets around the cake board too if you wish.

SUMMER PARTY

It's great to get together during the long summer holidays. An ideal finishing touch to a birthday sleepover (or before an essential shopping trip with friends) would be a brunch party. Take inspiration from other countries for party themes.

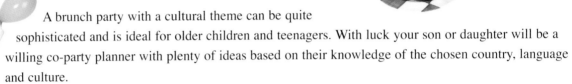

A brunch party with a cultural theme can be quite sophisticated and is ideal for older children and teenagers. With luck your son or daughter will be a willing co-party planner with plenty of ideas based on their knowledge of the chosen country, language and culture.

The USA's Independence Day on 4th July is great inspiration for a summer party. You don't necessarily have to be American to celebrate with red, white and blue and it's an easy theme to spark off ideas.

Encourage your guests to come in costume, representing the country – think of Ivy League-type sweatshirts or a sparkly Madonna urban cowboy look. It doesn't have to be full fancy dress, as any accessory such as a stars and stripes flag will help set the scene. Give out a small prize for the 'best dressed' guest.

BRUNCH PARTY

PETIT DEJEUNER FRENCH STYLE

Serve warm croissants and French sticks, continental-style jams, brioches, milky coffee served in bowls or breakfast cups, orange juice, ham and cheese, followed by fruit and yoghurts.

INDEPENDENCE DAY CELEBRATION

Provide muffins, waffles with maple syrup, bacon and eggs-over-easy or sunny-side-up, orange juice, fruit, tea, coffee or milk served in tall glasses or non-spill travel mugs (often given away free by coffee bars).

SETTING THE SCENE

• For both French and USA themes red, white and blue is the order of the day. Use plain white china with coloured bowls (France) or heavy diner-style china with oversized mugs and glasses (USA). Napkins can be plain red or blue.

• Paint a white sheet to look like the Tricolour or Stars and Stripes. Alternatively decorate the middle of a plain table cloth with a solid colour red or blue runner. For the 4th July, you can sprinkle paper stars along the runner or twirling ribbons in the style of cheerleaders.

• Finish with miniature flags stuck in traditional, glass cola bottles (USA) or small mineral water or fruit juice bottles (France) filled with sand for stability.

• Instead of placemats, buy a couple of copies of the Wall Street Journal, Le Figaro or other foreign newspaper and place these, folded under the plates.

• Place cards can be decorated with airmail stickers or foreign stamps or can be folded postcards with names written in the style of the theme, such as Monsieur Tom, La Belle Maria, Slick Ben and the Bikers, Anna T and the Pink Ladies.

• Don't forget to have appropriate music playing in the background – Rock'n'Roll from the 50s and 60s to create the atmosphere of an authentic diner or soulful jazz for the feel of the Parisian Left Bank.

• Goody bags are not essential for a brunch party, but if you wish to give guests a little souvenir, these can be placed next to their name cards on the table. Choose anything which is evocative of the theme country.

ACTIVITIES

Why not round off the party with an energetic game of baseball (or rounders) or a more leisurely game of boules? You could present the winning team with baseball caps or berets.

CLOWNING AROUND

This happy chappie will bring fun and smiles to the party. You could get the children to dress up and have a circus theme. Remember to reserve a tablespoon of uncooked cake mixture to bake the fairy cake for his head.

INGREDIENTS
20cm (8in) round sponge cake
(see page 17)
1 fairy cake
2 quantities buttercream, flavoured
with a few drops of vanilla
essence(see page 20)
Green food colour paste
1 meringue nest
Ice cream cone
Round colourful sweets
Strawberry bootlace sweets
2 trifle sponge fingers

EQUIPMENT
25cm (10in) round
cake board
Carving knife
Palette knife

TIP
If you can't find strawberry bootlaces,
use liquorice catherine wheels or pipe
a buttercream smile and strands on the
hat instead.

2 To make the clown, place the fairy cake onto the meringue. Glue in place with buttercream. Colour about 2 tablespoons of buttercream green and smear on top of the cake.

1 Split the cake horizontally into two or three layers and reassemble it filling the layers with vanilla buttercream. Spread buttercream around the outside. Place the cake to one side.

3 Push the ice cream cone into the hair. Using dabs of buttercream, stick two sweets onto the cone and a red one on the face to make his red nose.

4 Tie some strands of strawberry bootlace into a knot and stick on top of the cone. Bend a short length of bootlace into a smile and stick onto the clown's face. Use a little water if necessary to help it stick.

5 Place the clown in position on the cake. Cut two trifle sponge fingers down to size and stick into the cake for his arms.

6 Decorate the outside of the cake with sweets.

COOL CAT

This technique is called 'frozen buttercream transfer' is an easy way to make a design for the top of a cake. Because it is prepared 'off-cake', it doesn't matter if it goes wrong first time. If you don't have cling film to hand, you can use greaseproof paper instead.

Photocopy this design at 140% to create a template to trace

INGREDIENTS
20cm (8in) round sponge cake (see page 17)
1 quantity vanilla buttercream (see page 20)
1 quantity chocolate buttercream (see page 20)
White chocolate buttons
Black and pink or red food colour paste
500g (1lb 2oz) white marzipan
Strawberry bootlace sweet

1 Make the top design first. Enlarge and trace the cat design above onto greaseproof paper and place on a cake board. Place a sheet of cling film on top. Colour about 2 tablespoons of buttercream black and place into a piping bag fitted with a No 2 piping nozzle. Pipe over the outline. Keep the bag when you've finished for making the eyes on the mice later.

2 Fill in the outline using bags filled with different coloured icing. If you are using greaseproof piping bags, you don't need to use piping nozzles. Simply fold over the end of the bag to close it and to force the icing down towards the end. Then snip a tiny triangle off the end.

EQUIPMENT
25cm (10in) round cake board (for cake)
2 spare boards – any size, thick or thin (for top design)
Pencil
Greaseproof paper
Cling film
Piping bags (see page 22)
No 2 piping nozzle
Dressmaker's pin
Carving knife
Palette knife
Small paintbrush
Scissors

TIP
You can prepare your top design up to a month in advance and store it in the freezer.

3 Lay another sheet of cling film over the top of the design. Place a second cake board on top and gently squeeze together. Turn the whole thing over and remove the uppermost board. Using a soft circular motion, gently rub the buttercream through the cling film so that the icing fills all the gaps. Prick any air bubbles with a pin to remove them. Place in the freezer for at least two hours.

4 To prepare the cake, make sure the top of the cake is as flat as possible. Cut it in half and fill the middle with buttercream. Reassemble, place on the cake board and ice the sides and top with chocolate buttercream.

5 When the design is frozen, remove the cake board and peel away the *bottom* layer of cling film. Place the design on the top of the cake and peel away the *top* sheet of cling film.

6 Stick a circle of white chocolate buttons around the edge of the design to neaten the top of the cake.

7 Divide the marzipan in half. Colour one portion pink. To make a mouse roll about 20g ($^2/_3$oz) marzipan into a carrot shape. Make two tiny ball shapes for ears and stick onto the body (use a dab of water if necessary). Make a hollow in each ear with the end of a paintbrush. Make six mice of each colour.

8 Pipe three black dots on each mouse for eyes and nose. Insert a short length of strawberry bootlace for the tail. Stick the mice around the base of the cake. Stick additional buttons around the sides of the cake.

HALLOWEEN FUN

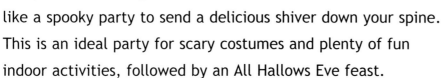

When it's the witching hour, there's nothing like a spooky party to send a delicious shiver down your spine. This is an ideal party for scary costumes and plenty of fun indoor activities, followed by an All Hallows Eve feast.

INVITATIONS

• Use purple card covered in gummed stars.
• Make simple potato prints in the shapes of moons, bones or a witch's hat and stamp onto coloured card.
• Stick wobble eyes on some round black circles of card and attach eight long legs (made from pipe cleaners or crêpe paper) to resemble a spider.
• Make a card out of tracing paper and cut a spook shape from white paper to slip between its ghostly covers (write the party details on the reverse).

Gruesome Gareth and Horrible Hattie invite all their spooky friends to a Halloween Party on 31st October at 5.30pm. Come dressed up as your favourite ghoul, goblin, wizard or witch.

RSVP or we'll send you a slimy toad!
Address
Telephone number

COSTUMES

Don't rush to buy ready-made costumes from a toy or party shop. Making your own devilish outfit is much more fun and cost effective. In many cases some face paints add the final touch to warty witches or smelly three-eyed monsters.

DEVIL

A 150cm (60in) square of red fleece provides a great cover up for little devils and is warm on chilly autumn nights. Add a scary rubber mask or make your own from a paper plate painted red with cut-out eyes and nose, plus some felt horns stuck to a hair band. Make the hair stand in peaks with some hair gel.

WIZARD

You don't have to go to college to be a wizard. Simply cut stars from some gold and silver card or orange felt and attach to a purple cloak. Decorate a paper cone hat with celestial stickers (use hair grips to secure or have an elastic loop under the chin). A length of dowel painted black, and with silver foil wrapped on the end becomes a magic wand and a hanging bat cut from a square of foam is essential for spells and experiments.

Wizard specs

Anyone can look like Harry with these glasses! Take two pipe cleaners. Twist to make a circle in the middle of each for the lenses. Twist two overlapping ends to form the bridge of the glasses. Trim any surplus. The other ends can be curved to fit over the ears. Make sure that there are no sharp ends before wearing.

WITCH

Wear anything black and make a long, slinky cloak from a square of skirt lining fabric – it's cheap, shiny and usually 140cm (54in) wide. A black bin liner will do as a dress if you cut out neck and arm holes. A black hat, wand and a mean expression are the only extras needed.

SETTING THE SCENE

• Use coloured card from art shops or crêpe paper, folded into zigzags and make garlands (like paper dolls) in the shape of pumpkins, black cats, scary spooks or bright green frogs.

• Attach small bat shapes to table lamp shades and fit low wattage bulbs to cast an eerie gloom and large shadows. An adult should supervise this before the party.

• Make or buy rustic twig stars and loop together with string, separating each star with a tiny apple to create a simple but effective garland.

• Cover furniture and the tea table with white sheets (or dye black using machine fabric dyes).

• Don't forget to have some spooky music playing to send shivers down your spine.

SPOOKY FOOD

Make edible place cards. Cut slices of gingerbread cake into thick chunks and ice on guest names with writing icing. If names are long, write initials only! This is a good activity for the children to do in advance.

After some active games or trick and treating, warm little monsters with a bowl of pumpkin, carrot or tomato soup served with starry toasts. Toast bread as usual (bread should not be too thick). Leave the toast to cool for a second and then use a large star cookie cutter to press out the toasts on a bread board.

CARVING PUMPKINS

These giant fruit are a traditional part of the Halloween fun (and food). Available in all shapes and sizes, they can be hollowed out and lit from the inside with a tea light. You must ask an adult to help you.

• First draw a simple design of eyes, nose and mouth on one side with a felt tip pen and a circle at the top.

• Ask an adult to cut out the top of the pumpkin and the outlines of the shapes using a small, sharp vegetable knife or craft knife.

• Circles can be easily created with an apple corer.

• Scoop out the flesh with an ice-cream scoop or melon baller.

• The flesh can be used for pumpkin soup or pies and the seeds toasted.

• Line up pumpkins in the window or on the garden path for a welcoming glow.

GAMES

SPOOKY SHADOWS

This is a good game for quietening everyone down before eating or leaving. Attach a white sheet on one wall. One of the children sits down on a chair facing the sheet. At the opposite wall of the room is a lamp on the table. All the players walk between the lamp and the guesser in turn. The guesser must recognize the players by their shadows (he/she must not turn around). The players try to change their shadows by hunching their shoulders, stooping or changing their appearance with a hat or false beard. The player who is recognized becomes the guesser in the following round. You can also play traditional shadow miming games.

THE WITCH'S RELAY

Divide the guests into two teams and have half of each team at either end of the room. The first player puts one of his/her feet into an empty bucket. Holding the bucket handle in one hand and a broom or besom in the other, the player must run to the other side of the room – it's harder than it looks! – and then pass the bucket and broom onto the next player. The first team to finish is the winner.

NEWTON'S LAW

Hang some apples (use windfalls) on strings from the ceiling. Divide the players into pairs and give one player in each team some scissors and the other player a hat. The first player in each pair cuts the apple string and the second player tries to catch it in the hat. The difficulty is that players cannot lift the hat off the floor! The pair which manages to gather the greatest number of apples wins the game. If played outside, tie the strings to trees or the washing line.

GOODY BAGS

Use squares of black felt or crêpe paper, quickly sewn or glued into sacks. Fill with any small gifts in suitable colours, plus an apple and orange. Other treats could include jellied monsters and lips, DIY wands, some awful jokes, plus craft materials for making pom pom spiders and pipe cleaner specs.

SPOOKY GHOST

Not too tricky and a treat to eat! For a really ghoulish surprise, mix a little green food colour into the cake mixture before baking!

EQUIPMENT
Carving knife
Palette knife
25cm (10in) round cake board
Rolling pin
28–30cm (11–12in) round dinner plate
Small sharp knife
Paintbrush

INGREDIENTS
Pudding bowl sponge cake
(see page 17)
1 quantity buttercream (see page 20)
Icing sugar for rolling out
500g (1lb 2oz) white ready-to-roll icing
15g (^{1}/2oz) black ready-to-roll icing
Red food colour paste (optional)
50g (1^1/2oz) grey-coloured coconut
(see page 23)
2-3 jelly snake sweets

1 With the widest part of the cake forming the base, split the cake horizontally two or three times and fill with buttercream. Stand the cake in position on the cake board and buttercream the outside of the cake. Do the sides first so that you can hold the top steady and avoid getting your fingers too sticky. Place the cake to one side.

2 Dust the worksurface with icing sugar and knead the ready-to-roll icing until it's pliable. Roll it out to a thickness of about 1cm (^{1}/4in) and place the dinner plate on top. Cut around the plate using a sharp knife to leave a large icing disc.

3 Lift the icing disc up and carefully place it over the top of the cake, allowing it to fall into folds. Make two 30g (1oz) ball shapes out of the leftover white ready-to-roll icing for eyes and stick these onto the ghost's face using little dabs of water.

4 Make three small black ready-to-roll icing balls and flatten two into discs for eyeballs and stick onto the eyes. Squash the other into an oval for his mouth.

6 Smear a little leftover buttercream around the cake board and carefully spoon the coloured coconut around the base of the cake. (The buttercream should help make it stick and not drop all over the table.)

7 Arrange the jelly snakes around the board and ghost. (A few dabs of water should be enough to keep them in place.) Finally, make a few little icing bones. First make a little white sausage shape. Then squash each end and, using a paintbrush, push a little dent into each end.

5 Add a tiny white ball to each eye to give the impression of highlights and a small ball of white for his nose. Paint in a few ghoulish blood vessels using a fine paintbrush and a little red food colour.

TIP
To save even more time, you might be able to find ghoulish eyeball-shaped sweets in the shops!

CRUNCHY MUNCHY MONSTER

This one is fun to cut! Watch out for low-flying krispies!

INGREDIENTS
1 pudding bowl cake (see page 17)
1 quantity chocolate buttercream (see page 20)
150g (5oz) milk chocolate
90g (3oz) cereal e.g. rice krispies
50g (2oz) coloured mini marshmallows
2 large marshmallows
50g (2oz) white mini marshmallows
2 chocolate buttons
2 jellybeans
25g (1oz) coloured sweets
7-8 chocolate sticks

EQUIPMENT
Carving knife
Palette knife
Heatproof bowl
Wooden spoon
25cm (10in) round cake board

1 Slice the pudding bowl cake two or three times horizontally and sandwich the layers together with buttercream. Place the cake in position on the cake board and spread a thick coating of buttercream around the outside.

2 Melt the chocolate in a heatproof bowl in a microwave which will take between 1-3 minutes depending on the power of your machine. Alternatively, place in a heatproof bowl on top of a saucepan of simmering water. Do not get any water into the chocolate.

3 Stir in the cereal and add the coloured marshmallows.

4 When the mixture feels fairly cool, press handfuls against the sides of the cake. Leave a space for the face. Beware – you will get sticky!

5 Use two regular marshmallows for eyes and a line of white mini marshmallows for teeth. The buttercream on the cake should hold them in place but use a little more if you need to. Add chocolate button eyeballs and jellybean eyebrows. Fill in the rest of the face with more krispies.

6 Cover the cake board too with krispie mixture and push chocolate sticks into the head. Finish him off with some extra coloured sweets, sticking them in place with dabs of buttercream.

SPIDER CAKE

Chocolate cake was used as a base in this design so that the web showed through the buttercream. However you can use another flavour if you prefer. When making the sponge, save a couple of teaspoons of cake mixture to bake a fairy cake for the spider's body.

INGREDIENTS
18cm (7in) round chocolate cake
(see page 17)
1 chocolate fairy cake
1 quantity vanilla buttercream (see page 20)
I strand raw dried spaghetti
Milk and white chocolate buttons
Liquorice bootlace or Catherine wheel
Currants
2 sheets rice paper

EQUIPMENT
Carving knife
20cm (8in) square cake board
Palette knife
Kitchen paper
Scissors

1 Level the top of the cake and turn it upside down. This will give the cake a flat surface. Slice it in half and fill the centre with buttercream. Place the cake on the board, reassemble and spread buttercream around the sides and top.

2 Holding the spaghetti strand upright, draw a series of lines fanning out from the centre of the cake for the web. Icing will collect on the end so have some kitchen paper handy to wipe it off. Then draw slightly curved connecting lines between them.

3 Press a line of chocolate buttons around the top and bottom edges of the cake. Place to one side.

4 To make the spider, take the fairy cake out of its wrapper and turn it upside down. Stick two white chocolate button eyes in position with dabs of buttercream. Add two currants for pupils and stick in place with buttercream.

6 To make a fly, cut wings out of rice paper. Place a currant and wings onto the web. Gently press everything into the buttercream so that it's nice and secure. Make as many flies as you want – depending upon how hungry your spider is!

TIP
Buttercream the sides first so you can hold the top without getting too sticky.

5 Cut a short length of liquorice for his mouth. Moisten it slightly with water so it becomes tacky and stick it into position. Cut eight liquorice strips for legs. Push one end of each leg into the cake. Place him into position on the cake and stick the other end of each leg into the icing.

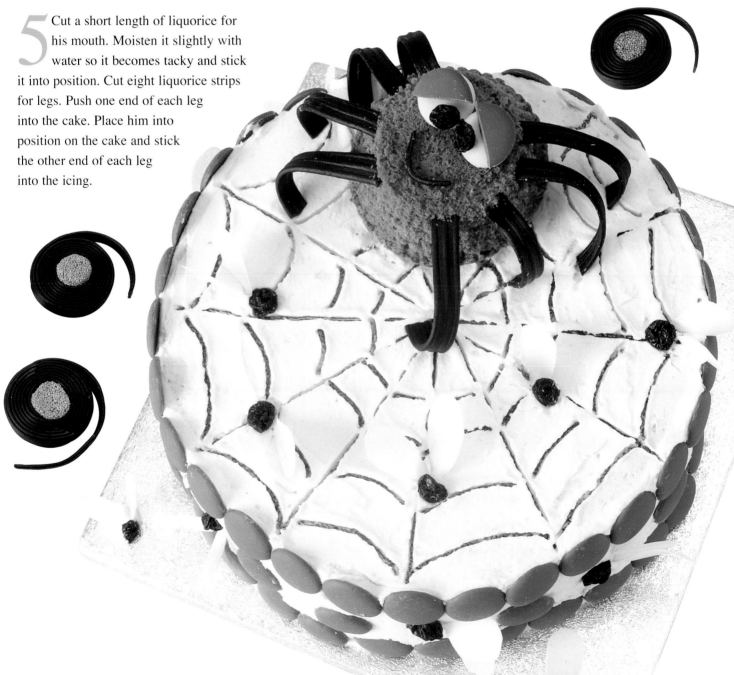

COUNTDOWN PLANNING

With a little forward planning, on the big day you can concentrate on fun rather than organization.

THROUGHOUT THE YEAR

• Buy seasonal partyware in the sales to save money. Start up a party box and stockpile small gifts or give-aways for goody bags. Remnants of exotic fabrics, nets and trimmings can also be stored for fancy dresses. A materials box with crêpe paper, sticky tape, string, balloons and a pump is also useful as a standby.
• Note down ideas for themes – get inspiration from children's books, films and magazines.

SIX WEEKS BEFORE

• Decide on the date and time for the party and theme if applicable. Remember the party doesn't have to be on the actual birthday.
• Book outside venues/entertainers if necessary (you may need longer for popular choices).

FOUR WEEKS BEFORE

• Decide on the party guests.
• Make and write the invitations. For younger children, print the party details and let them write in the guest's name and sign it. Include your telephone number for RSVPs and a deadline for replying.

TWO–THREE WEEKS BEFORE

• Hand out or post the invitations.
• Start making any props or costumes.
• Rope in the help of grandparents or creative friends. Children love playing make believe with extra stand-ins, especially when they are in character (Sheriff and Big Chief Bread-and-Butter for example).
• Buy small prizes or raid your party box.
• Decide on the birthday cake.
• Decide what type of food you will have. Remember to keep it simple, have small portions and consider any allergies (nuts etc).

ONE WEEK BEFORE

• Phone any guests who haven't replied (children do tend to put invitations into their school backpacks and not tell anyone until the day before the party!).
• Buy all non-perishable party food, drink and candles.
• Buy or record any special music you need. With any musical games, have a pre-recorded tape prepared, so there are no gaps as the tracks change.
• Assemble goody bags.

ON THE MORNING

(or day before if possible)
• Try to get the birthday child out of the way for a few hours as you'll work a lot faster!
• Decorate your home, garden and tea table.
• Gather together any props you need for the games.
• Prepare food.

PARTY RECORD

Keep a party record in a notebook for useful reference. Include details of themes, games, numbers of guests, party food and other bright ideas that you can use again in future years.

TEMPLATES

Jolly Roger skull and cross bones
see page 34

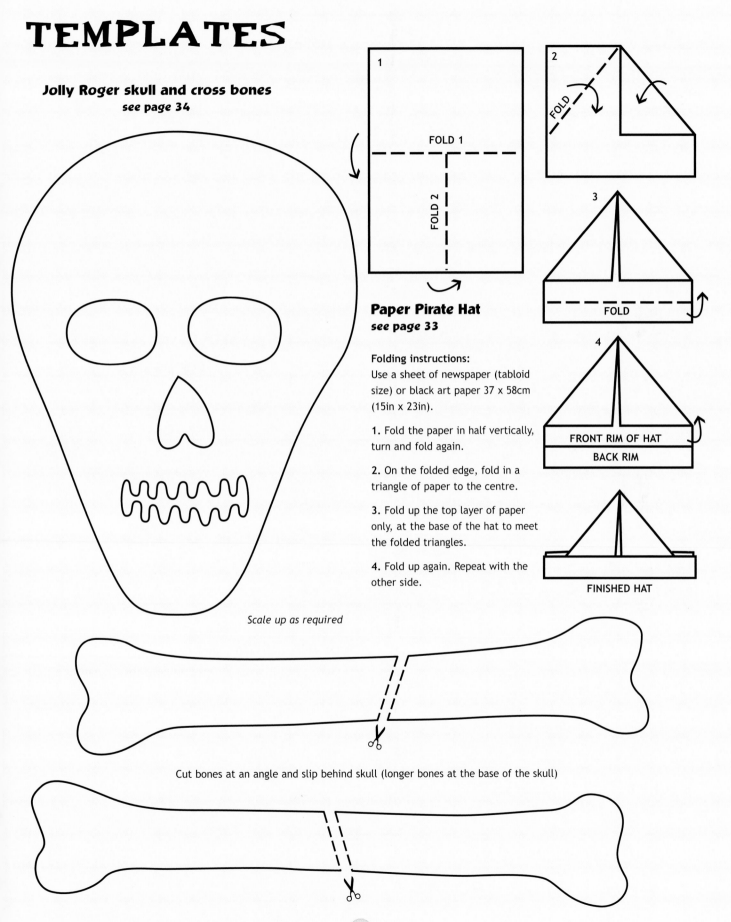

1 FOLD 1

FOLD 2

2 FOLD

3 FOLD

4 FRONT RIM OF HAT

BACK RIM

FINISHED HAT

Paper Pirate Hat
see page 33

Folding instructions:
Use a sheet of newspaper (tabloid size) or black art paper 37 x 58cm (15in x 23in).

1. Fold the paper in half vertically, turn and fold again.

2. On the folded edge, fold in a triangle of paper to the centre.

3. Fold up the top layer of paper only, at the base of the hat to meet the folded triangles.

4. Fold up again. Repeat with the other side.

Scale up as required

Cut bones at an angle and slip behind skull (longer bones at the base of the skull)

127

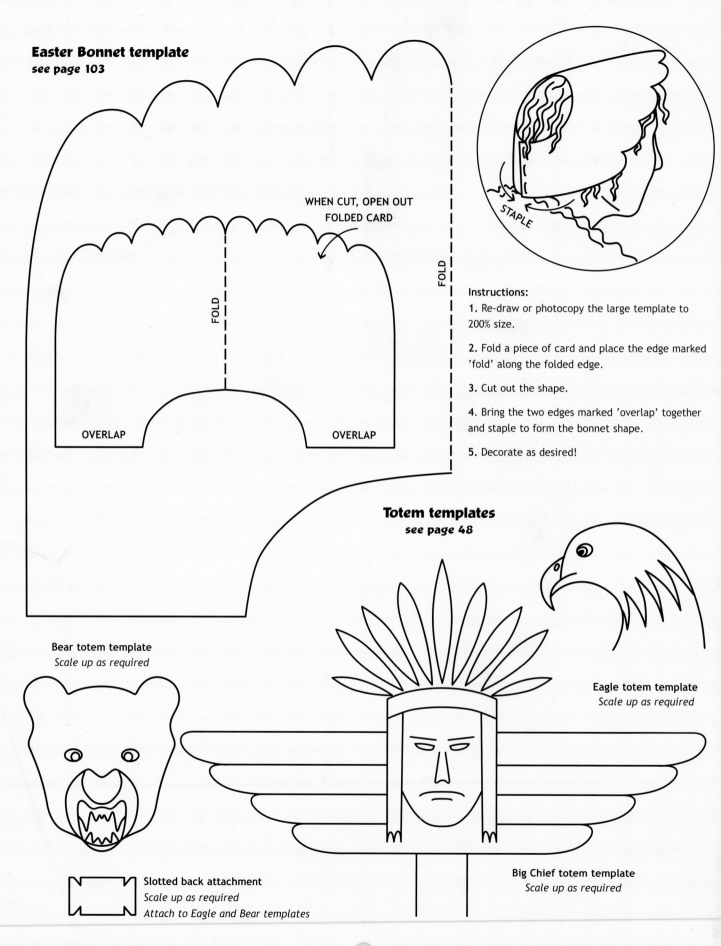

Easter Bonnet template
see page 103

WHEN CUT, OPEN OUT
FOLDED CARD

FOLD

FOLD

FOLD

OVERLAP

OVERLAP

STAPLE

Instructions:

1. Re-draw or photocopy the large template to 200% size.

2. Fold a piece of card and place the edge marked 'fold' along the folded edge.

3. Cut out the shape.

4. Bring the two edges marked 'overlap' together and staple to form the bonnet shape.

5. Decorate as desired!

Totem templates
see page 48

Eagle totem template
Scale up as required

Bear totem template
Scale up as required

Big Chief totem template
Scale up as required

Slotted back attachment
Scale up as required
Attach to Eagle and Bear templates

128